THE TRIUMPH OF
INTERNATIONALISM

Issues in the History of American Foreign Relations

Series Editor: Robert J. McMahon, The Ohio State University

In this series

The Color of Empire:
Race and American Foreign Relations
Michael L. Krenn

Crisis and Crossfire:
The United States and the Middle East Since 1945
Peter L. Hahn

Intimate Ties, Bitter Struggles:
The United States and Latin America Since 1945
Alan McPherson

The Triumph of Internationalism:
Franklin D. Roosevelt and a World in Crisis, 1933–1941
David F. Schmitz

THE TRIUMPH OF
INTERNATIONALISM

Franklin D. Roosevelt and a World in Crisis,
1933–1941

David F. Schmitz

Potomac Books, Inc.
Washington, D.C.

Library of Congress Cataloging-in-Publication Data
Schmitz, David F.
The triumph of internationalism : Franklin D. Roosevelt and a world in crisis, 1933–1941 / David F. Schmitz. — 1st ed.
p. cm. — (Issues in the history of American foreign relations)
Includes bibliographical references and index.
ISBN 978-1-57488-930-7 (hardcover : alk. paper) — ISBN 978-1-57488-931-4 (pbk. : alk. paper)
1. United States—Foreign relations—1933–1945. 2. Roosevelt, Franklin D. (Franklin Delano), 1882–1945—Political and social views. 3. Internationalism—History—20th century. 4. United States—Foreign relations—1933–1945—Sources. 5. Internationalism—History—20th century—Sources. I. Title.
E806.S349 2007
327.73009'043—dc22

2007006175

Potomac Books, Inc.
22841 Quicksilver Drive
Dulles, Virginia 20166

First Edition

10 9 8 7 6 5 4 3 2 1

To my parents,
Mary O. and David A. J. Schmitz,
and to my aunts and uncles,
Kathleen and Andrew J. Schmitz Jr.,
Brother Donald Schmitz,
Helen and Richard Schmitz,
Sister Sabyna Schmitz,
Lily and James Schmitz,
Eileen and Andrew Kindbergh, and
Florence and Richard Burns

CONTENTS

ILLUSTRATIONS

SERIES EDITOR'S NOTE

FROM THE BIRTH OF THE AMERICAN REPUBLIC in the late eighteenth century to the emergence of the United States as a fledgling world power at the end of the nineteenth century, the place of the United States within the broader international system of nation-states posed fundamental challenges to American and foreign statesmen alike. What role would—and could—a non-European power play in a Eurocentric world order? The combination of America's stunning economic transformation and two devastating world wars helped shatter the old European order, catapulting the United States into a position of global preeminence by the middle decades of the twentieth century. Since the mid–1940s, it has become common to refer to the United States as a superpower. Since the collapse of the Soviet Union, its only serious rival, and the concomitant end of the Cold War, it has become common to label the United States as the world's lone superpower, or "hyperpower," as a French diplomat labeled it in the late 1990s.

By any standard of measurement, the United States has long been, as it remains today, the dominant force in world affairs—economically, politically, militarily, and culturally.

The United States has placed, and continues to place, its own indelible stamp on the international system while it shapes the aspirations, mores, tastes, living standards, and sometimes resentments and hatreds of hundreds of millions of ordinary people across the globe. Few subjects, consequently, loom larger in the history of the modern world than the often uneasy encounter between the United States and the nations and peoples beyond its shores.

This series, *Issues in the History of American Foreign Relations*, aims to provide students and general readers alike with a wide range of books, written by some of the outstanding scholarly experts of this generation, that elucidate key issues, themes, topics, and individuals in the nearly 250-year history of U.S. foreign relations. The series will cover an array of diverse subjects spanning from the era of the founding fathers to the present. Each book will offer a concise, accessible narrative, based upon the latest scholarship, followed by a careful selection of relevant primary documents. Primary sources enable readers to immerse themselves in the raw material of history, thereby facilitating the formation of informed, independent judgments about the subject at hand. To capitalize upon the unprecedented amount of non-American archival sources and materials currently available, most books will feature foreign as well as American material in the documentary section. A broad, international perspective on the external behavior of the United States, one of the major trends of recent scholarship, will be a prominent feature of the books in this series.

It is my fondest hope that this series will contribute to a greater engagement with and understanding of the complexities of this fascinating—and critical—subject.

Robert J. McMahon
Ohio State University

ACKNOWLEDGMENTS

I THANK ROBERT MCMAHON, THE SERIES EDITOR, AND DON JACOBS at Potomac Books for including my book in this series. Bob provided guidance in the conceptualization of the work and support throughout the process. Don's editorial skill brought greater clarity and precision to the book. It has been a pleasure to work with both of them.

The archivists at the Franklin D. Roosevelt Presidential Library have been unfailingly professional and helpful during all of my trips there over the years. In particular, Bob Clark and Mark Renovitch went out of their way in providing assistance for the research for this book. Similarly, the staff at Sterling Library, Manuscripts and Archives, Yale University, provided expert advice on Henry L. Stimson's papers.

This work would not have been possible without the generous support from Whitman College, which allowed me to travel to the various archives to conduct research and to employ, through the Lewis B. Perry Summer Research Scholarship Program, David Young as a research assistant. David assisted me in locating documents at the Roosevelt Library and in the public record and with numerous other tasks. Lucy Palmersheim provided assistance with the research on lend-lease, particularly in the *Congressional Record*. Maura Flaherty, while working for me on a different project, helped me with some final research on public opinion. Kathy Guizar of Image Management again provided me with expertise in preparing the photographs for the book.

Warren Kimball read the entire work, asked probing questions, and provided an incisive critique that improved the book. Lloyd Gardner directed my first research on Franklin Roosevelt and the 1930s, and he continues to provide wise counsel and a model of scholarship. I am grateful that he has shared with me over the past twenty-five years his vast knowledge of Franklin Roosevelt's foreign policy, his friendship, and his support.

The love and support of my wife, Polly, sustained me through the difficult periods of our lives that coincided with the writing of this book. It simply would not have been finished without her. Our visit together to the Roosevelt Library and Museum in Hyde Park, New York, was the highlight of writing this work. My children Nicole and Kincaid remind me all the time why studying and explaining the past is so important.

I dedicate this work to my parents, Mary O. and David A. J. Schmitz, and to my aunts and uncles, Kathleen and Andrew J. Schmitz Jr., Brother Donald Schmitz, Helen and Richard Schmitz, Sister Sabyna Schmitz, Lily and James Schmitz, Eileen and Andrew Kindbergh, and Florence and Richard Burns. They came of age during the Great Depression and World War II, and they all made the sacrifices President Roosevelt asked of the nation as it went to war in 1941. The achievements of the time and of that generation were their achievements as much as the president's.

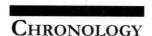

CHRONOLOGY

1931

September 18   The Japanese destroy part of the South Manchurian Railroad at Mukden, beginning Japan's conquest of Manchuria.

1932

January 2   The Japanese Army takes Chinchow in Manchuria, thus securing its control over the province.

January 7   The Stimson Doctrine of nonrecognition of Japan's conquest of Manchuria is announced.

November 8   Franklin D. Roosevelt is elected president of the United States.

1933

January 30   Adolf Hitler is appointed chancellor of Germany.

March 4   Roosevelt is inaugurated as president.

March 23   The Enabling Act gives Hitler the powers of a dictator.

October 21   Germany leaves the League of Nations.

1934

August 19   Hitler becomes the Führer of Germany, thereby combining the offices of president and chancellor after the death of President Paul von Hindenburg.

1935

March 16   Hitler introduces military conscription, thus violating the disarmament clauses of the Treaty of Versailles.

August 31   President Roosevelt signs the first Neutrality Act.

October 3   Italy invades Ethiopia.

1936

March 7   German forces occupy the Rhineland.

May 9   Italy completes its conquest of Ethiopia.
July 17   The Spanish Civil War begins.

1937
July 7   Japan invades China and thus begins the war in the Pacific.
October 5   President Roosevelt delivers his "Quarantine Speech"
             in Chicago, Illinois.
November 6   Italy signs the Anti-Comintern Pact with Germany and
             Japan.

1938
March 13   Austria is annexed by Germany.
September 29 The Munich agreement cedes Czechoslovakia's Sude-
             tenland to Germany.

1939
March 15   Germany takes the rest of Czechoslovakia.
March 28   The Spanish Republic is defeated.
August 23   Germany and the Soviet Union sign the Nazi-Soviet
             Nonaggression Pact.
September 1 Germany invades Poland.
September 3 Great Britain and France declare war on Germany.
September 5 President Roosevelt announces U.S. neutrality.

1940
April 9   Germany invades Denmark and Norway.
May 10   Germany invades France, Belgium, Luxembourg, and
             the Netherlands.
May 10   Winston Churchill becomes the British prime minister.
June 10   Italy declares war on France and Great Britain.
June 19   Henry L. Stimson is named U.S. secretary of war.
June 22   France surrenders.
September 3 The destroyers-for-bases deal is announced.
September 16 President Roosevelt signs the Selective Service Act.
September 27 The Tripartite Pact (Axis) is signed by Germany, Japan,
             and Italy.
November 5   Roosevelt is reelected president for a third term.

1941
March 11   President Roosevelt signs the Lend-Lease Act.
June 22   Germany invades the Soviet Union.
July 24   Japan occupies southern Indochina.
July 26   The United States freezes Japanese assets in America
             and establishes a complete embargo on trade.
August 14   President Roosevelt and Prime Minister Churchill agree
             to the Atlantic Charter.
December 7   Japan attacks Pearl Harbor.

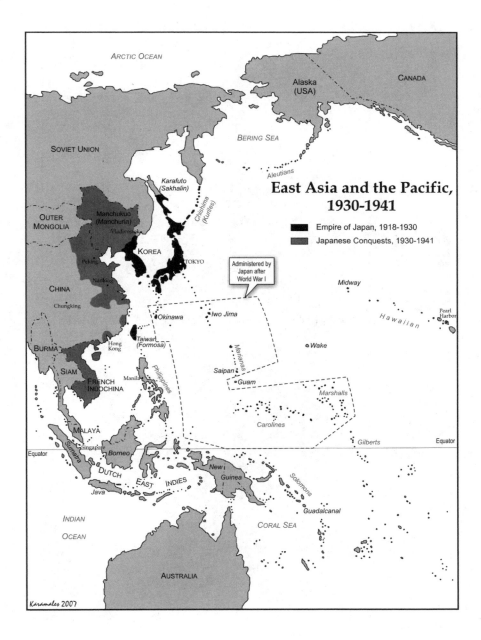

ARCTIC OCEAN

Alaska
(USA)

CANADA

BERING SEA

SOVIET UNION

Aleutians

Karafuto
(Sakhalin)

**East Asia and the Pacific,
1930-1941**

OUTER
MONGOLIA

Manchukuo
(Manchuria)

Chishima
(Kurlles)

███ Empire of Japan, 1918-1930

███ Japanese Conquests, 1930-1941

Vladivostok

KOREA

Midway

Peking

TOKYO

Administered by
Japan after
World War I

CHINA

Nanking

Okinawa

Iwo Jima

Hawaiian

Pearl
Harbor

Chungking

Taiwan
(Formosa)

Wake

BURMA

Hong
Kong

Marianas

SIAM

FRENCH
INDOCHINA

Manila

Philippines

Saipan

Guam

Marshalls

MALAYA

Carolines

Gilberts

Equator

Equator

Singapore

Sumatra

Borneo

DUTCH

EAST

INDIES

New
Guinea

Solomons

Java

INDIAN

OCEAN

CORAL SEA

Guadalcanal

AUSTRALIA

Karamales 2007

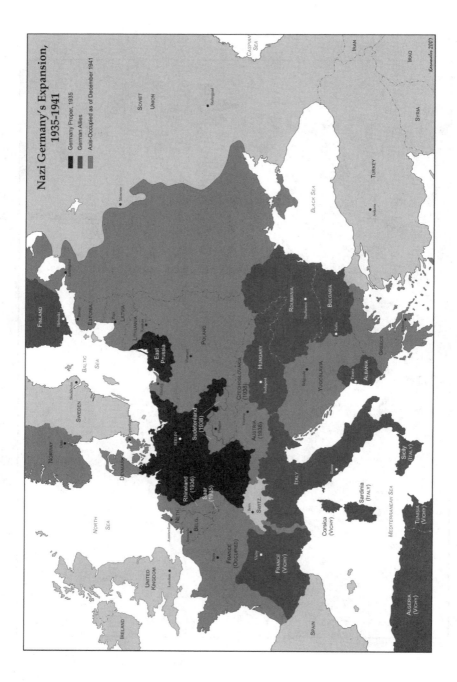

Nazi Germany's Expansion,
1935–1941

Germany Proper, 1935

German Allies

Axis-Occupied as of December 1941

INTRODUCTION

WHEN U.S. PRESIDENT FRANKLIN D. ROOSEVELT TOOK OFFICE in March 1933, he faced a series of unprecedented crises that tested the nation's institutions and threatened its security. While Roosevelt initially devoted most of his attention and efforts during his first term in office to finding a solution to the Great Depression, by the end of the decade that concern was overwhelmed by the escalating threats from Nazi Germany and Imperial Japan. Roosevelt was forced to confront the long-standing American sentiment against U.S. intervention in foreign wars that grew in response to the international crisis of the 1930s. Thanks to traditional policies such as the Monroe Doctrine and hemispheric defense and a belief that neutrality, trade, and freedom of the seas were the proper concerns of American foreign policy, and reinforced by disillusionment with American participation in World War I, the failure of the Versailles Treaty, a growing peace movement, and the related problems of wartime loans and the economic crisis that culminated in the Great Depression, people from all parts of the United States held to neutrality and noninterventionism. Over the course of his first two terms in office, Roosevelt gradually overcame these popular sentiments and moved the nation toward accepting the internationalist definition of America's role in the world and national security. In doing so, the president reshaped the public's understanding of the national interest and defense, and Americans came to accept the necessity for war in Europe and Asia in the defense of U.S. interests. Thus Roosevelt established the basis for post–World War II American foreign policy.

During the 1930s and early 1940s, therefore, Americans debated and fought over the extent of the U.S. role in the world and the use of power as an instrument of policy. The passage of the Neutrality Act of 1935 marked the triumph of the noninterventionist position that held sway until the decade's end. By 1940, however, with the president's reelection for an unprecedented third term in office, Roosevelt's internationalist view of the United States as a world leader, with its power and influence extended globally, basing its defense on preparedness and collective security, working with allies and international organizations to promote American values and institutions, and willing to intervene when necessary to protect U.S. interests and carry out its goals, took hold and guided the United States into World War II.

During Roosevelt's first term in office, the issues of international trade, the establishment of the Good Neighbor policy toward Latin America, and the emerging disputes in Europe dominated the president's foreign policy agenda. Connecting these events was the Roosevelt administration's quest to use foreign policy to support reform efforts at home by creating greater international trade and stability that would assist economic recovery and provide for the peaceful resolution of disputes. An internationalist, Roosevelt supported American involvement in world affairs and international organizations and believed the United States should play a leadership role not just in its traditional sphere of influence, Latin America, but globally as well, to promote peace, prosperity, and liberal values. Yet, the president was aware of the political restraints on his ability to act and, therefore, sought to protect American interests abroad short of direct political involvement outside the Western Hemisphere. He was unwilling to risk raising controversial foreign policy issues and incurring the isolationists' wrath at the same time he pursued his New Deal initiatives at home. Thus, Roosevelt's initial response to the crisis in Europe was to continue to use trade and economic means to influence events. He adopted a policy of economic appeasement toward Germany, while seeking ways to support China and deter further Japanese aggression in East Asia.

To understand Roosevelt's response to German aggression, it is necessary to see the international crisis of the 1930s not just as a great power conflict but also as a battle among competing ideologies and political systems: liberalism, fascism, and communism. The Roosevelt administration spent much of the 1930s trying to determine which power or system was the greatest threat to the West and the United States and could come to dominate Europe. In other words, the Roosevelt administration was most concerned with how the United States and the Western democracies could meet the challenge posed by Nazi Germany and fascism without the Soviet Union's support. Roosevelt understood that a French-British alliance without either the United States, which was politically impossible at the time owing to the rejection of the Treaty of Versailles, or the Soviet Union would be too weak to contain Germany on the continent. A policy of confrontation with Hitler's government in the mid-1930s, therefore, would have meant accepting a popular front and cooperation with both Moscow and the political left in Europe. Within this context Roosevelt developed his policy of economic appeasement in the hope of moderating German demands and countering the Third Reich's expansion without making political commitments or cooperating with the Soviets.

By 1937, Roosevelt had begun to turn more of his attention toward foreign policy and the growing threats to world peace. Europe was always of greater importance to the president, but the Japanese invasion of China threatened long-standing American interests and policy in East Asia and brought forth efforts short of war by Roosevelt to curb Japan's aggression. After Japan's attack on China in 1937 Roosevelt took on the enormous task of changing public opinion to accept his vision of internationalism and U.S. world leadership. Although the president had earlier recognized Japan as an ideological and strategic rival and protested Japan's aggressive behavior in Manchuria, the U.S. response until 1937 had not gone any further than nonrecognition. Responding to full-scale war in China, Roosevelt gave notice that he saw Japan's actions as a threat to American interests and that he would oppose a Japanese empire in East Asia. His "Quarantine Speech" marked this shift. In this speech, the president laid the foundation for increased American involvement abroad and established the doctrine of just war as the basis for national security.[1]

Simultaneously, German revisions of the Versailles Treaty and increasing belligerency exposed the shortcomings of both the noninterventionist position and economic appeasement and led to efforts by Roosevelt to increase American aid to Great Britain and to redefine American foreign policy around an expanded internationalist definition of national security and preparedness for war. Roosevelt, invoking the arguments of just war and the defense of democracy against totalitarianism, slowly but surely moved the nation away from a limited view of hemispheric defense and neutrality toward intervention against German and Japanese aggression in the defense of national security and American values. The president's proclamation of the United States as the "great arsenal of democracy" on December 29, 1940, and as the upholder of the four freedoms—freedom from want, freedom from fear, freedom of speech, freedom of religion—on January 6, 1941, in conjunction with the passage of the Lend-Lease Act in March 1941, marked the culmination of this process.[2] By this time, Nazi Germany's aggression had led to its control of almost all of Europe. With Great Britain the only force standing between the United States and Nazi-dominated Europe and England's survival uncertain, all qualms of cooperation with the Soviet Union were swept aside when Hitler ordered the invasion of Russia in June 1941. By the time the Japanese attacked Pearl Harbor, the American people were prepared to take up the burden and sacrifices of World War II. Thus, Roosevelt moved the nation beyond a view of hemispheric defense, increased trade, and neutrality to an internationalism that accepted the risks of global intervention, political alliances, and the necessity of the use of American power abroad as the only means to provide both prosperity and peace.

This book, therefore, seeks to demonstrate that the old categories of debate about Roosevelt's policy during the 1930s, isolationism versus intervention, are misleading. To say American policy was isolationist is a distortion of reality as the United States was always involved with the rest of the world through trade, cultural contacts, immigration, finance, wars, and interventions in other nations. Only in terms of joining the League of Nations or taking on political obligations in Europe did isolationism have meaning. In addition, the debates of the 1930s were about more than whether or not the United States would again become a direct and partisan participant in solving Europe's problems. The debate that developed between the non-interventionists and President Roosevelt was over the fundamental nature of American foreign policy, a battle between neutrality outside of the Western Hemisphere and an internationalism that accepted a global role for the United States.[3] In his efforts to move the nation away from a reliance on hemispheric defense and neutrality to a definition of national security based on alliances, just war, and global leadership, the president made the case that Nazi Germany and Imperial Japan, in their efforts to control Europe and Asia, were direct threats to the United States. But, Roosevelt argued, it would take more than just force to keep the nation safe. Only the spreading of American values and institutions would bring real security to the nation, and thus ideology was as important a component of policy as geopolitical concerns.

Many historians, most notably Robert Divine, John Wiltz, and Justus Doenecke, argue that Roosevelt was an isolationist who only slowly changed his views in the late 1930s in response to events abroad. They cite the president's actions during the London Economic Conference and the signing of the neutrality acts as evidence. Robert Dallek, while agreeing in large part, argues that Roosevelt trimmed his internationalist sails when he became president and acted as a nationalist and isolationist until 1938–1939. Others, even some who see the president as an internationalist, accept this verdict and ignore the early period altogether when discussing Roosevelt's policy.[4]

This understanding needs to be revised. The president's seemingly isolationist acts were matters of political necessity and greater concern for domestic events. Examining the whole period, the context and continuity for the crucial decisions of 1939–1941 demonstrate that Roosevelt was consistent in his outlook on international affairs and acting as quickly as he thought politically possible. As a result, Roosevelt's decisions and actions leading up to World War II were critical in America's relations with the world, as important as those made at any other time in twentieth-century U.S. foreign policy. Moreover, they not only brought the nation into the war, they shaped the thinking of the next generation of American leaders and Cold War policy after the war.

CHAPTER 1

THE PERILS OF REPUBLICAN
INTERNATIONALISM

WORLD WAR I, OR THE GREAT WAR AS IT WAS CALLED prior to the 1940s, did not solve any of Europe's major problems and created a whole set of new problems both there and in Asia. That the roots of World War II can be found in the Great War, therefore, is correct in two interrelated ways. First, President Woodrow Wilson's compromises at Versailles allowed the Allies to impose a punitive peace against Germany that bred the resentment and the backlash Adolf Hitler exploited to gain power. Second, the collapse of the old order in Europe led to the emergence of a new, unstable international system that included the ideological challenges of bolshevism and fascism in Europe and brought Japan's threats to the status quo in East Asia. Thus, the international crisis of the 1930s was shaped by the failures of the Versailles Treaty, the flawed internationalism of the 1920s, and the Great Depression.

These events, which shaped the thinking of both the American public and the Roosevelt administration, provided the context for Franklin D. Roosevelt's foreign policy and the limits to the actions he could take. The American disillusionment with the Great War and rejection of the Treaty of Versailles led to a refusal throughout the 1920s to make any political commitments in Europe. Instead, American foreign policy emphasized trade, neutrality, and hemispheric defense. America never, however, adhered to a policy of isolationism. American policymakers pursued American economic interests, adjustments to Europe's fiscal obligations, disarmament agreements, and intervention in the Western Hemisphere to maintain order

1

and protect American interests. The conservative internationalism of the Republican administrations, therefore, favored expanding trade and invest-ment but remained based on the traditional American worldview that limited political involvement outside of the Western Hemisphere, main-tained protective tariffs despite the United States being a creditor nation, and held to a vision of defense of American interests predicated on the buffer of the Atlantic and Pacific oceans. It is essential to survey world events and U.S. policies from 1919 to 1933 to understand the issues, prob-lems, and restraints that Roosevelt confronted when he became president in March 1933.

The Versailles System

As Daniel M. Smith has noted, World War I marked a "great departure" for the United States.[1] For the first time the United States had fought a war in Europe, joining a coalition of forces to defeat Germany. President George Washington in his Farewell Address had warned the nation of tying itself to any foreign countries or influences. Twelve years later, Thomas Jefferson spoke about the dangers of entangling alliances and the need to maintain America's freedom of action in the world. The Monroe Doctrine, announced in 1823, with its warning to Europe against efforts to reclaim any colonies in the Western Hemisphere and pledge by the United States to remain neutral in Europe's disputes, was in line with Washington's and Jefferson's ideas and policies. This was not isolationism, as the United States, driven by notions of Manifest Destiny, remained an expansive nation throughout the nine-teenth century and, through the quest for markets and raw materials, be-came actively involved in the affairs of East Asia and the nations to its south. The self-imposed restriction was on joining forces with European nations and making commitments that hampered the U.S. ability to act with-out having prior obligations.

President Woodrow Wilson partially overcame this legacy when he took the nation to war in 1917. But even Wilson was mindful of the caution preached by the nation's founding fathers and made it clear that the United States was an "associated" power and not an ally so as to not be committed to the treaties and agreements the Europeans had already reached concern-ing the war's outcome. To be sure, Wilson sought, with his Fourteen Points, to establish a new international order in which the United States would play a central and crucial role in postwar Europe through the League of Nations. In this effort, he moved further in breaking with the past than many Americans wanted. Once the president arrived at Versailles to negotiate with the British, French, and Italians, he found it difficult to translate his ideals into reality and was forced to compromise on many parts of his program in order to reach an agreement.

The Treaty of Versailles failed to create a stable postwar order. Its harsh provisions against the defeated nations, exclusion of revolutionary Russia, and failure to gain ratification in the U.S. Senate all contributed to the difficulties of the postwar years. The terms of the treaty humiliated Germany by stripping the nation of land and colonies, disarming it, imposing large reparations payments to the Allies, and including a war guilt clause that asserted that Berlin alone was responsible for the war. All of this saddled the new postwar Weimar Republic with significant economic burdens and linked it with the treaty and defeat. Even while vigorously trying to enforce the provisions of Versailles, France remained wary of a revival of German power. Paris, therefore, took other measures to make sure its neighbor could not invade again, as it had twice in the last fifty years, through enormous defense spending, including the construction of the defensive Maginot line, and forming alliances with Poland and Czechoslovakia in an effort to encircle and contain Germany. Surely one root of Hitler's rise to power in the early 1930s, along with the Great Depression, was German anger with the terms of the treaty and the Nazi leader's promises to remedy the injustices and return Germany to its former—and, in Hitler's view, rightful—power and glory. While this was not readily apparent at the time, and certainly no one at the outset of the 1920s could have predicted the rise of fascism in Germany or the nature of the Third Reich, it is clear that the Versailles system helped bring the change about.

The profound political changes caused by the decline of the old order after World War I compounded the problems created by the Versailles Treaty. The most obvious manifestation of the decline was the collapse of four major empires—the German, Austrian-Hungarian, Ottoman, and Russian—which changed the political landscape in Eastern Europe and brought forth new states. On the right, the upheaval of the war years and postwar instability led to the emergence of fascism in Italy and Mussolini's taking of power in 1922. In Russia, the fall of the czar and the Russian Revolution culminated in the Bolsheviks coming to power in 1917. The formation of the Soviet Union created a state based on a social system fundamentally different from and antithetical to that in the West, the public ownership of the means of production. Along with failed revolutionary efforts in Hungary,

Germany, and elsewhere, and a growing political left throughout Europe, the Bolshevik Revolution created fear of the spread of communism beyond Russia and early efforts to contain the danger.

Indeed, one source of Wilson's compromises at Versailles was the fear of bolshevism. In addition to the concern about a revived Germany, there was the danger of communism and the spreading of the 1917 Bolshevik Revolution in Russia toward the West. The United States had joined Great Britain, France, and Japan in sending troops to Russia in opposition to the Bolsheviks in a failed effort to drive them from power. After the withdrawal of American troops, Washington refused to recognize the new regime in Moscow. Moreover, during the 1920s, the Western European democracies formed alliances with and provided aid to the newly formed states of Eastern Europe to provide a bulwark against the spread of bolshevism westward and to isolate the Soviet Union.

From the American perspective, the postwar period was not supposed to be this way. Wilson had taken the nation to war promising a "peace without victory," a settlement based on his Fourteen Points that would make the world safe for democracy and bring an end to international conflict. Even when the president was met with opposition from the European leaders and forced to compromise on the terms for peace, Wilson believed that the League of Nations would be able to redress the most negative aspects of the Treaty of Versailles and usher in a new international order based on cooperation, compromise, and common interests. Conflicts would be prevented by disarmament, arbitration of disputes, and collective security against aggressor nations. Thus, President Wilson believed that American interests would best be served through the use of the League of Nations to provide collective security as well as peaceful resolutions of international disputes.

The question of American membership in the League of Nations, however, was a divisive one in the United States. While most internationalists in both parties supported membership in the League, many Republican leaders had significant concerns about article X of the League's covenant and its provision that all member nations were obligated to "respect and preserve as against external aggression the territorial integrity and existing political integrity of all members of the League." They found the provision impractical for the United States as the American people would not honor this commitment to collective security everywhere in the world or allow the decision on whether or not to go to war to be taken away from Congress.

Led by Elihu Root, Republican moderates offered a series of reservations for ratification of the Treaty of Versailles, most notably that the United States could disclaim all obligation to honor any articles it found objectionable even while ratifying the treaty and becoming a League member. This was unacceptable to Massachusetts senator Henry Cabot Lodge, the chair of the Senate Foreign Relations Committee, who led the attack against the treaty and the moderate revisions by proposing a series of amendments designed to defeat the purpose of U.S. membership in the League. Lodge was not an isolationist. Rather, reflecting the conservative internationalist perspective, he believed that American should trade with Europe but that U.S. security was best achieved through hemispheric defense and avoiding any entangling alliances or political commitments that would involve the United States in the inevitable next "European war." Lodge's opposition to the Versailles Treaty and the League of Nations was anchored in the old traditions of American foreign policy and represented the main objectives of isolationist sentiment in the nation. With Wilson unwilling to compromise and the question of League membership politically unpopular, the Treaty of Versailles was never ratified.

Many Americans were disillusioned with the sacrifices of World War I and were determined not to repeat what they saw as a mistake. Thus, the attitude of the American people was isolationist when it came to European political affairs. Still, the period of 1921–1929 was one of hope and optimism for American leaders. Even though the Senate had rejected the Treaty of Versailles, Republican policymakers such as Secretary of State Charles Evans Hughes, Secretary of Commerce Herbert Hoover, and Secretary of State Frank Kellogg were confident that the United States would play a constructive and positive role in world affairs and were determined to redress the fundamental problems they saw in the international system that threatened peace and American interests.

Throughout the 1920s, the key problem that faced American foreign policymakers was creating stability and order in the world while promoting American interests and avoiding making any U.S. political commitments, particularly in Europe. Republican internationalists sought to overcome the U.S. rejection of the Treaty of Versailles by increasing American cooperation with Europe and remedying the shortcomings of the postwar order by negotiating a series of disarmament and debt-reduction agreements aimed at lessening tensions and increasing international trade. American officials believed such actions would reduce the danger of war, provide greater security and stability, and promote American trade and prosperity.

The United States emerged from the Great War as the world's leading creditor, greatest industrial producer, and most powerful nation. In conducting American foreign policy during the 1920s, Republican leaders drew on several lessons from World War I that guided their diplomacy. First, the United States could not be isolated from the rest of world and had to assume some of the responsibility of world leadership. With the League of Nations politically unacceptable as the vehicle for solving international problems, the only route to peace was through political stability and increased international trade, which would create prosperity and great power cooperation. Second, the war had proved that the world's economies were interdependent and that American prosperity was tied to Europe's economic recovery. Central to Europe's economic health was Germany. This meant that adjustments would have to be made to the economic provisions of the Versailles Treaty to facilitate and maintain Germany's recovery from the war. The punitive reparations agreements had to be reduced to achieve the dual goals of peace and prosperity. Finally, the billions of dollars in war debts owed to the United States by the Allies were a drain on their economies, and they too had to be reduced. While Washington refused to directly link reductions in reparations with lowering the war debts, the policy pursued sought the dual reduction of these financial obligations to promote economic recovery and greater international trade. Although Republican leaders continued to reject political involvement in Europe's affairs and disputes, the United States used its economic power to assist Europe's recovery and to create a cooperative international system that would be safe from the concomitant dangers of war and revolution.

Republican officials saw the agreements in the Versailles Treaty and France's intransigent insistence concerning any revisions in the reparations to be paid by Germany as the main problems blocking Europe's full recovery from the war. They feared that given this burden, Germany would never be able to recover fully from the war and would thus hold up recovery for all of Europe and create political instability and the possibility of revolution. France's extensive defense spending and formation of alliances to surround Germany with hostile states compounded these concerns. As a nation that did not ratify the Treaty of Versailles and a non-League member, Washington could do little in the face of Paris's refusal to entertain any treaty revisions and efforts to fully collect reparations from Berlin.

Germany, however, was unable to meet its obligations on time, and this created economic uncertainty in Europe and political tensions with its former adversaries. In 1923, France, saddled with an enormous debt from its military excesses, sent its forces into the Saar Basin in western Germany to force payments at the point of the bayonet. German officials refused to cooperate, and the French occupation soon turned disastrous for both France and Germany. France, deeply in debt and unable to compel payment, saw its international credit ruined by a drastic devaluation of the franc. At the same time, the German economy was beset with hyperinflation. The arrangements made at Versailles would have to be modified.

This crisis allowed Washington to step in and revise the financial agreements on American terms. Charles Dawes, a leading banker, led an American delegation to Europe to stabilize the French and German economies, impose new schedules for reparations payments, and promote greater trade. To get Paris to agree to a downward revision of reparations, American banks extended new loans to France to restore the value of its currency and to offset its loss in revenues from Germany, and negotiators promised to discuss a reduction of France's war debts. Loans were also made available to Germany to stabilize its currency, to finance recovery, and to increase its ability to import products and produce goods.

The Dawes Plan, along with the negotiated agreements to lower all European nations' war debts, had the desired impact on Europe's economy. Germany's economy recovered, and Berlin resumed reparations payments. France's economy, along with the rest of Europe's, stabilized, and U.S. trade with Europe increased to $2.6 billion annually, double its prewar value. All of this was fueled by loans from the United States that totaled over $1.3 billion to Germany alone. American dollars lubricated the system of European finance and appeared to provide the solution to the negative consequences of the Versailles Treaty. Thus, the vision of a shared prosperity based on cooperation, mutual interests, and the free movement of capital and goods seemingly took hold in Europe. Neutrality and limited American commitments did not appear contradictory to American interests in promoting European stability, prosperity, and trade.

The positive impact was evident in political events as well. The Locarno Pact, signed by Germany, France, and Belgium, with Great Britain and Italy as guarantors, pledged each nation to respect the existing political borders in Western Europe and augured for a peaceful settlement of future disputes. The Young Plan of 1929 represented a further reduction in reparations and war debts owed and seemed to signal an agreement between the United States and the powers in Europe that prosperity and security were best guaranteed in an integrated economic system and cooperative political order. Without making any political commitments and working from outside of the League of Nations, American officials believed they had successfully used American economic strength to create peace and prosperity in Europe, thus validating their conservative internationalist approach to securing American interests abroad.

The Washington System

From Washington's vantage point, the final piece in rearranging the international puzzle that had been poorly put together at Versailles was disarmament. Republican policymakers in the 1920s believed that a significant reduction in the world's arsenals and the reduction of the amount of capital used for weapons would lessen the chances of international conflict, promote economic development, and persuade countries, both in Europe and Asia, to settle their disputes through negotiations. The primary vehicle for these efforts was the so-called Washington System: the United States negotiated a series of treaties that reduced the size of existing navies and limited future naval shipbuilding, provided guarantees to China's territorial integrity, upheld the principles of the Open Door policy of free trade, and sought to meet Japanese needs by integrating Japan into a U.S.-led international trade system, thus eliminating Tokyo's desire to expand its territories in East Asia.

Since the announcement of the Open Door policy at the end of the nineteenth century, the United States had worked to promote free trade, access to markets, and the territorial integrity of China against efforts by Europeans and the Japanese to gain concessions and possibly divide China into colonies. By the end of World War I, China was in disarray. Technically the Kuomintang Party (KMT) governed the country, but warlords controlled large areas while foreign nations held extraterritoriality arrangements over various port cities. The Washington System was in part designed to have all nations respect Chinese sovereignty once the KMT established effective control over the nation, but the KMT never established control. In pursuit of this goal, the United States was the first nation to recognize the KMT as China's government.

Japan posed the greatest threat to China. The first non-Western nation to industrialize, Japan faced significant problems. It lacked many of the raw materials necessary for a fully developed industrial economy and had to import most of its fuel, minerals, and other basic items. Simultaneously, the

Japanese home islands could not produce enough food to feed its population; this further forced the nation to rely on imports. Taking a cue from the Western powers, the Japanese colonized Korea and Taiwan and gained control over parts of China in order to have access to raw materials and places to settle Japanese citizens abroad.

The United States and Japan, therefore, had conflicting aims regarding China as Washington sought to protect the Open Door policy and Chinese nationalism while Tokyo sought to increase its influence on the mainland. These difficulties were furthered by Japan's dissatisfaction with the Versailles Treaty and its failure to gain control over the former German concessions in China. The Washington System was designed to recognize legitimate Japanese security interests and needs for markets and raw materials while preventing Japan from taking direct control over large parts of China. Naval limitations and recognition of the Open Door policy gave the United States what it sought while Japan, growing ever more dependent on the United States for oil, iron, and other products, agreed to pursue its security and prosperity through cooperation with the United States.

Secretary of State Charles Evans Hughes, who served from 1921–1924, designed the Washington System and oversaw its implementation. At the opening of the Washington Naval Conference in December 1921, Hughes declared that the United States would scuttle all the ships it had under construction and called upon the others in attendance, most notably Great Britain, France, Italy, and Japan, to follow suit. Having seized the initiative, Hughes was able to gain agreements that limited the allowed tonnage of capital ships at a fixed ratio of United States and United Kingdom 5: Japan 3: France and Italy 1.25. Thus, Japan was allowed the largest single navy in the Pacific, as the United States and Great Britain maintained two ocean navies, and could not be threatened by a single power. Two other treaties, the Four-Power Treaty and the Nine-Power Treaty, followed these agreements. The former, signed by France, Great Britain, Japan, and the United States, called for consultations by the signatories should problems arise in East Asia, while the later, which included Belgium, China, Italy, the Netherlands, and Portugal along with the four powers, guaranteed China control over its territory and formally recognized the Open Door policy, thus in theory ensuring all nations' access to China's market and foreign trade.

Hughes and other Republican leaders were convinced that these agreements would prevent a dangerous and costly arms race while providing for Japan's economic and security needs, ending its efforts to expand,

and ensuring political stability in East Asia. The three treaties signed in Washington had great appeal in the United States as they promised to provide a road away from war in the settlement of disputes. Throughout the 1920s, the system appeared to function as Hughes designed it, with the KMT gaining greater control over China, and Japan obtaining its necessary supplies through international trade, particularly with the United States, which bought more than 40 percent of Japan's exports and sent oil, scrap iron, lumber, food, and other essential items to Japan. The Open Door vision of mutual prosperity stemming from free trade, international cooperation, interdependence, and disarmament would, Washington believed, serve the interests of all nations and make it unnecessary for the United States to formally join the League of Nations or take up political and military commitments to protect its global interests and security.

Toward the Good Neighbor Policy

Latin America represented the one area of the world in which the United States had extensive political as well as economic involvement and Washington exercised a dominant influence through its military power and economic might. The defeat of Spain in 1898 led to the taking of Puerto Rico and the establishment of a protectorate over Cuba through the Platt Amendment, which allowed for American intervention in Cuban affairs. During the next decade, Theodore Roosevelt secured American control over the Panama Canal Zone and issued the Roosevelt Corollary to the Monroe Doctrine, which declared that the United States had the right to intervene in the nations of Latin America if instability in the region threatened order and American interests or if the nations to the south failed to meet their international obligations. This exercising of an international police power, as Roosevelt phrased it, soon led to the dispatch of American forces at different times over the next three decades to Cuba, the Dominican Republic, Haiti, Honduras, Mexico, and Nicaragua and to the establishment of financial protectorates over Cuba, the Dominican Republic, and Haiti.

The Monroe Doctrine, according to American officials, had created a "special relationship" between the United States and Latin America, and Latin America was seen, Henry L. Stimson explained in 1931, as the area of the world "most vital to our national safety, not to mention our prosperity."[2] Instability in the region was, therefore, a serious problem that made it incumbent upon Washington to find a means to maintain the order necessary to protect the Panama Canal and American economic interests. Many in Latin America did not see it this way and argued that American policy was one of imperialism designed to allow Washington to dominate its neighbors to the south, a claim American policymakers denied. In the words of Charles Evans Hughes, the United States sought "prosperous, peaceful, and law abiding neighbors with whom we can cooperate to mutual advantage." Yet, recurring unrest, in Hughes's opinion, forced the United States to intervene. "It is revolution, bloodshed and disorder that bring about the very interposition for the protection of lives and property that is the object of so much objurgation."[3]

The interventions in Cuba, the Dominican Republic, Haiti, Mexico, and Nicaragua did not, however, create more stable governments and secure American interests. Rather, these military missions created continuous resentment and hostility toward the United States throughout the region and confirmed in the minds of many the charges of U.S. imperialism. In response to U.S. aggression, feelings of nationalism and opposition grew among Latin Americans. Hughes sought to remedy this problem through treaties that would establish order and protect American interests. In December 1922, the secretary of state sponsored a conference with the nations of Central America in Washington to discuss regional stability, guarantees for the protection of property, and methods for combating revolutions. All the nations in attendance agreed that they would not recognize any governments that resulted from coups d'etat or revolutionary takeovers. Although the United States did not sign the Central American treaty, it agreed to honor its provisions. Hughes hoped that this would remove the necessity of continued U.S. intervention. He believed that withholding Washington's recognition would deter unconstitutional seizures of power, thereby providing for stability in the region, protection for the existing governments, the promotion of trade and economic development.

The outbreak of civil war in Nicaragua in 1926 showed the ineffectiveness of the 1923 treaty and brought a renewal of American military intervention. The U.S. intervention in Nicaragua was met with extensive criticism in Latin America and the United States, which compelled the Coolidge administration to search for another method to resolve the conflict without the use of force. Toward that end, Washington sent Henry L. Stimson to Nicaragua in April 1927 to mediate an end to the fighting and prevent future outbreaks of civil war. Stimson quickly concluded that the current government had to be retained to uphold the Central American treaty and preserve constitutional order and that the United States had to supervise the next series of elections in Nicaragua to guarantee that they were fair.

The United States, however, could not simply use more troops to ensure the government's continuation in power until the next elections. This would fail to solve the more fundamental problems of governmental legitimacy while generating even more opposition to the United States and continuing the cycle of revolution. The answer, Stimson concluded, was to create a Nicaraguan force, the National Guard, to ensure stability once U.S. forces left without further American intervention. The creation of the local army solved the dilemma of how to maintain order and protect American interests without having to deploy the marines.

Recognizing that American actions had aroused more anger than support, Stimson, upon becoming secretary of state in 1929, sought to bring an end to all U.S. military interventions in Latin America. In December 1928, Undersecretary of State J. Rueben Clark, a prominent international lawyer, sent Secretary of State Frank B. Kellogg a lengthy memorandum that analyzed the Roosevelt Corollary and concluded that it was a misapplication of the Monroe Doctrine. In early 1930, Stimson officially repudiated the Roosevelt Corollary when he published the Clark Memorandum. Although the rejection of Theodore Roosevelt's claim did not completely disavow intervention, it took away the justification for it based on the Monroe Doctrine and set the groundwork for Franklin Roosevelt's Good Neighbor policy. In addition, Stimson removed most of the remaining American forces in the region as the United States looked toward indigenous groups or individuals to maintain order and provide a favorable environment for American business. As was the case in many of these nations, these individuals turned out to be military leaders and dictators who imposed order with U.S. support.

The Great Depression

The onset of the Great Depression, starting with the crash of the New York Stock Market in October 1929, began the unraveling of the economic arrangements in Europe and the Washington System in East Asia. The interrelatedness of the world's industrial economies almost guaranteed that when the U.S. economy collapsed the rest of the world would follow. In a foolish, yet politically popular, effort to protect American markets, Congress passed in 1930 the Hawley-Smoot tariff, which established the most restrictive trade barriers in the nation's history. Other nations quickly followed suit. European nations closed off their empires to outside commerce and international trade dropped by over 50 percent at the beginning of the 1930s, making it more difficult for American producers to sell abroad and for other nations to earn dollars to pay back their debts to the United States. The Great Depression now represented a worldwide near-collapse of capitalism.

The Dawes and Young plans were successful because of the flow of American capital, loans, and credits. The collapse of the stock market and the interruption of trade cut off the dollars that made the system work and brought a return to the economic chaos of the early 1920s. In May 1931, the Austrian central bank failed, precipitating a banking crisis throughout Central Europe. Germany soon announced that it was no longer able to meet the payments on its debts to foreign nations, and this created the danger of a general default on all international debts. As conditions worsened, social strife increased in many European nations, thus raising the fear of political instability, the repudiation of all international obligations, and the spread of communism. To meet this crisis, the United States announced a one-year moratorium on all intergovernmental debts and a standstill agreement on private debts to strengthen Germany's finances and protect all of Europe's banks and credit. These efforts failed to solve the underlying economic problems, and the downward cycle continued on both sides of the Atlantic. In this context, Hitler's call for a repudiation of Versailles gained the Nazis new supporters as Germany began to reject international cooperation as a means to protect its security and prosperity.

The onset of the Great Depression undercut the Washington System and had a devastating impact on relations with Japan. As access to American funds evaporated in the wake of the stock market crash and the Hawley-Smoot tariff cut Japan's exports to the United States in half, the system quickly unraveled. With Great Britain, France, and Holland closing off their empires to foreign trade, Japan found itself unable to acquire many of the materials necessary for its economy. The militarist faction in Japan, which had always questioned the idea of cooperation with the West, gained the upper hand. It set out to create an empire that would be self-sufficient and did not depend on other nations for its prosperity and well-being. From the Japanese perspective, the United States supported the Open Door only when it gained from the arrangement and violated the policy when it served Washington's purposes. The militarists decided that Japan's prosperity and security were better gained through unilateral action, and in September 1931 Japan began to take control over Manchuria by force.

From the outset, the United States opposed the Japanese conquest and sought to cooperate with the League of Nations on measures to deter Japan's move and to support China. President Herbert Hoover opposed economic sanctions, fearing that they would lead to war, and it was clear that the League nations were not going to take any action. Short of war, there was seemingly little Washington could do to stop Japan. Yet, Secretary of State Stimson did not want to condone Japanese aggression and its violation of the Nine Power Treaty. The only viable option was nonrecognition of Japan's conquest and the mobilization of public opinion in opposition to such actions. The Stimson Doctrine, announced on January 7, 1932, stated that the United States "cannot admit the legality of any situation *de facto* nor does it intend to recognize any treaty or agreement . . . which may impair the treaty rights of the United States . . . including those which relate to the sovereignty, the independence, or the territorial and administrative integrity of the Republic of China, or to the international policy relative to China, commonly known as the open door policy."[4]

Stimson did not believe this declaration would check Japan's aggression or bring about a reversal of its course. But nonrecognition could effectively serve American interests as a moral weapon designed to express the opposition of the United States and its people to the Japanese action. Moreover, the secretary of state hoped it would help shape world opinion on the issue and serve as a means to reassure China and others that the United States was not abandoning its interests in East Asia. The Japanese had to be made to realize that their success in Manchuria notwithstanding they still had to contend with the opinion and power of the rest of the world. With the world too divided and unwilling to take action against Japan, the Stimson Doctrine, with its refusal to sanction Japan's dismemberment of China, was the best alternative available to awakening the world to the potential dangers that lay ahead if aggression was not checked. Certainly, with the economic problems at home mounting, the American public would go no further at that time. Nonrecognition was correct, but it was also insufficient for upholding international agreements and deterring aggression.

Conclusion

When Roosevelt was elected president in November 1932, the nation and the world were in a state of crisis. On all fronts, the new president faced difficult, complex problems. In January 1933, Hitler came to power in Germany bringing forth a direct challenge to the Versailles System. Simultaneously, the political left was growing stronger in parts of Europe as many questioned the ability of capitalism and liberal democracies to provide a solution to the crisis and looked toward the Soviet Union as a possible alternative. In East Asia, the Washington System had collapsed under the weight of Japan's conquest of Manchuria, and no agreements were in place to check Tokyo's ambitions. Unrest was also spreading in Latin America as the economic crisis brought new miseries and calls for change. While he would not be starting from scratch, Roosevelt faced a series of unprecedented problems that would fully test his abilities to lead the nation.

After his election, Roosevelt met with Stimson to discuss the state of the world and America's policies on various issues. On Europe, the president elect was circumspect about what he would do concerning the economic crisis and the political unrest on the continent. He refused to endorse any actions Hoover might take on debts, disarmament, or other measures to cope with the depression, and Stimson thought that he underestimated the extent of the problems. This was not the case, as Roosevelt was well

Franklin D. Roosevelt in his Ford Model A roadster, 1933.
Franklin D. Roosevelt Library

aware of the importance of Europe and international trade to the United States and of the destabilizing impact of the Great Depression but refused to restrict his own freedom of action before taking office. In any event, Roosevelt's first priority was to address the problems at home, and he was not willing to make foreign policy issues of equal importance or take controversial actions abroad as he prepared to launch his New Deal program.

Concerning East Asia and Latin America, Roosevelt noted his agreement with current policy. He approved of Stimson's actions regarding Manchuria and publicly endorsed the Stimson Doctrine. Reversing his own earlier position on the necessity and value of intervention in Latin America, Roosevelt also agreed with the Clark Memorandum and the policy of removing American forces from Latin American nations as a means to reduce tensions and provide for greater cooperation with these nations. Roosevelt built upon these actions when he announced the Good Neighbor policy toward Latin America at the beginning of his presidency.

Roosevelt's first term in office, however, saw few successes in addressing these problems. As the Great Depression deepened, many Americans, following President Hoover's lead, blamed much of the problem on Europe and developments overseas. Disillusioned with Versailles, isolationist sentiment hardened into a determination to avoid any involvement with problems outside the Western Hemisphere. Roosevelt, too, wished to concentrate on problems at home and his domestic reforms. But he believed that American economic recovery and prosperity was linked to international trade and he sought avenues to increase U.S. participation in world affairs. Still, by the end of his first term in office, events abroad came to demand more of Roosevelt's time and energy than he had ever envisioned.

CHAPTER 2

NEUTRALITY ASCENDANT

FRANKLIN ROOSEVELT BECAME PRESIDENT AT THE NADIR of the Great Depression. Unemployment was at least 25 percent and millions of Americans were underemployed; bank failures and business closings were daily occurrences; and breadlines were ubiquitous scenes in all major cities. Even though Roosevelt had an abiding interest in international affairs and the world presented many difficulties, his attention and initial efforts were by necessity devoted to launching his New Deal program, restoring confidence and faith in American institutions, and implementing reforms to solve the nation's problems. In his inaugural address on March 4, 1933, Roosevelt barely mentioned foreign policy. He did acknowledge that international trade was important but noted that it was a secondary concern at the moment. "I shall spare no effort to restore world trade by international economic adjustment," the president declared, "but the emergency at home cannot wait on that accomplishment."[1] Still, international relations could not be ignored, and the president sought to secure American interests in the world and to create an international environment that would aid in the recovery from the Great Depression.

Signaling the importance that international trade would hold in making foreign policy, Roosevelt appointed Cordell Hull as his secretary of state. A senator and former congressman from Tennessee, Hull was well known for his advocacy of lower tariffs and free trade. It was axiomatic to Hull that breaking down economic barriers and increasing international trade would lead to prosperity and peace, while high tariffs and nationalistic economic policies bred conflict and war. It was, Hull wrote, "virtually impossible to develop friendly relations with other nations in the political sphere so long as we provoked their animosity in the economic sphere." The free flow of trade, he reasoned, would raise every nation's standard of living "thereby eliminating the economic dissatisfaction that breeds war." In his memoirs, the secretary of state neatly summarized his view when he noted that, when war came, the nations that the United States had negotiated new trade agreements with were, with few exceptions, allies and none were foes. "The political line-up followed the economic line-up."[2]

During his first term in office, Roosevelt's policy was dominated by the issues of international trade and economic recovery, the Good Neighbor policy toward Latin America, and emerging political tensions in Europe and Asia. The Roosevelt administration sought greater international trade to aid economic recovery at home and to promote stability abroad. The concern over international issues was heightened by the growing appeal and power of fascism on the right and communism on the left, and the questioning of liberalism, capitalism, and democracy engendered by the Great Depression's spread in all parts of the world. It was not clear in what direction the upheaval would go, and American leaders were greatly concerned about continued instability and the spread of left-wing movements.

Roosevelt's thinking about the world beyond the United States was conventional for a man of his time, class, and background. Having traveled to Europe eight times as a child and teenager, he was Eurocentric in his outlook, and he continued to visit the continent as an adult until he was stricken with polio. Educated at elite schools with a classical curriculum, including Groton, Harvard, and Columbia Law, he saw himself as a cosmopolitan thinker and knowledgeable about the world and America's role in it. As a young man he was influenced by the sense of noblesse oblige instilled in him at Groton, and from his fifth cousin Theodore Roosevelt he gained a patrician's sense of obligation of service by those, as he saw it, who were best able to lead the nation. Roosevelt also shared his generation's ethnocentrism and belief in the necessity of leadership of the world by Western nations. Unflaggingly optimistic, Roosevelt was also confident in his own judgments and outlook, and he assumed that because he was a reasonable person, guided by democratic and Christian values and assisted by other logical and reasonable people, that the leaders of other nations would concur with his understanding of events and issues. When they did not agree with him, he assumed it was because of their own flaws or their racial inferiority. Roosevelt believed that American values and institutions were universal and that other people desired them and would adopt them if they had the opportunity. Thus, Roosevelt was an internationalist who consistently worked to expand America's role in the world and U.S. cooperation with Europe. While his contraction of polio led to a greater empathy for others within the United States, it never lessened his conviction that foreign nations benefited from their relationships with the United States and its ways and that the United States should take up the role of a world leader.

President Franklin D. Roosevelt with his secretary of state and free-trade advocate, Cordell Hull. Franklin D. Roosevelt Library

Before Roosevelt became president, his most extensive experience with foreign affairs was as assistant secretary of the navy under President Woodrow Wilson. He supported at the time the various American military interventions in the Caribbean basin in order to impose stability in the region, protect American economic interests, and bring uplift to the local inhabitants. His exaggerated boast as the Democrats' 1920 vice presidential candidate that he wrote Haiti's constitution reflected this attitude as well as his confidence in his own abilities. As an internationalist and because he believed in a larger U.S. role in the world, he was an early supporter of American entry into World War I and campaigned for the adoption of the Treaty of Versailles and membership in the League of Nations.

Given the enormity of the international crisis of the 1930s, Roosevelt had to consistently adapt and adjust his policies even while he never questioned his core internationalist positions or confidence that he could find a solution and all could be worked out. Indeed, his optimism and view that solutions were available to all problems and that he was dealing with rational leaders blinded him until late 1937 to the full extent of Hitler's expansionist desires and the fundamental evil of his regime and to Japan's ambitions in East Asia and the limits of deterrence against such a state. Thus, his first term in office lacked any urgency when it came to addressing the problems of growing international tensions and renewed international aggression that the Great Depression and the collapse of the 1920s international system brought forth.

Restraints on Policymaking

In making foreign policy at the outset of his term, a number of factors limited Roosevelt's ability to take action. While experimentation and change were called for at home, it was not a time for new initiatives abroad, and policies were pursued to enhance the status quo, not challenge it. This was consistent with the parameters of American internationalist thinking at the time. During the 1920s, American leaders became accustomed to influencing events and securing U.S. interests mainly through American economic power without making any political commitments or being involved in the League of Nations. Roosevelt continued this approach as a safe course of action. The domestic depression made it dangerous to raise controversial foreign policy issues and add them to the political debates over New Deal reforms of the time, particularly given the widespread sentiment against the

League of Nations and American involvement in European political affairs. While the United States was never an isolationist nation, public opinion was isolationist in terms of wanting to avoid American involvement in another European war.

This isolationist sentiment stemmed from the traditions of American foreign policy going back to the first days of the nation. George Washington and Thomas Jefferson had both warned against entangling alliances and involvement in Europe's political battles. The War of 1812 was fought in large part over the rights of neutrals to trade freely. The Monroe Doctrine was possible and effective because of the two oceans that separated the United States from the other great powers, and that geographic security had allowed for westward expansion across the North American continent with little opposition from those powers. The Open Door policy, originally announced at the end of the nineteenth century to protect American trade and interests in China, was designed to allow the United States the benefits of international trade and access to markets and raw materials without the political costs of empire.

While U.S. foreign policy was rooted in neutral rights and the defense of American shipping, World War I had marked a departure in many ways from these traditions as Americans went to Europe to fight to make the world, in Wilson's words, safe for democracy. Another major, overlapping restraint on Roosevelt's policy, therefore, was the Great War legacy. By the 1930s, it was unclear to most people what the United States had gained from its participation in World War I. The most notable outcomes of the war were bolshevism in Russia, continued political quarreling in Europe, the emergence of fascism, and an economic depression. Bestsellers such as Erich Maria Remarque's *All Quiet on the Western Front*, published in 1929 in the United States, provided a chilling indictment of the brutality and wastefulness of World War I and a desire to avoid a repeat at practically all costs.

What many Americans feared was involvement in another war in Europe that promised so little for the United States. While some were indeed isolationists who sought to cut the United States off from the world, most are better characterized as proponents of nonintervention and neutrality. Their disillusionment was fueled by a series of publications, such as the book *Merchants of Death* by Helmuth Carol Engelbrecht and Frank Cleary Hanighen and George Seldes's *Iron, Blood and Profits*, which were both published in 1934 and claimed that the United States was manipulated into entering the Great War by a conspiracy of bankers who had lent great sums to the Allies and wanted to protect their investments and munitions makers who benefited from the fighting and government purchases of their deadly products.[3] In March 1934, *Fortune* magazine ran an article titled "Arms and the Men" that claimed the munitions makers operated on the motto "when there are wars, promote them; when there is peace, disturb it."[4] These "Merchants of Death," noninterventionists argued, were the only people to profit from the war.

German and Italian actions also served to fuel the drive for new legislation to keep America out of war. Germany withdrew from the League of Nations and announced in March 1934 its plans for rearmament. In December of that year, Italy sought to expand its colonial empire, and Italian troops clashed with Ethiopian forces along the Ethiopian border raising the fear of war. Congress was deluged with letters and editorials calling for action to prevent bankers and arms makers from dragging the nation into another war. In response, the Senate established a special committee to investigate the munitions industry.

The "Merchant of Death" interpretation of the origins of U.S. entry into World War I gathered great strength during the Senate's investigation of the munitions industry, headed by Republican Senator Gerald P. Nye of North Dakota, and led to the passage by Congress of a series of neutrality acts designed to prevent a repeat of the events leading up to the Great War. The Nye Committee hearings on why the United States went to war in 1917 reached the same conclusion as the sensational publications that led to its formation: that bankers and arms merchants were responsible for American entry into World War I. This understanding became codified in law with the passage of the first neutrality act in 1935. The legislation stated that if the president found a state of war existed, the shipping of arms to belligerent nations and the transportation of war matériel on American ships would be prohibited. The next year a prohibition of loans to belligerents was added to the legislation, and in 1937, a "cash-and-carry" clause, designed to avoid the problems of loans and the carrying of goods on neutral ships, was added that would allow nations at war to purchase munitions in the United States as long as they paid for them in full and transported them on their own ships.

The Roosevelt administration opposed these restrictions and sought greater flexibility in neutrality legislation that would allow the president to impose an arms embargo against aggressor nations only. Roosevelt and Hull agreed with the goal of keeping the United States out of war if possible, but the president and secretary of state believed that inflexible neutrality could embolden potential aggressors who would not have to fear American support to any nation and, therefore, the president noted, "might drag us into war instead of keeping us out."[5] Moreover, legislation lacking discretionary power, Hull argued, would work against the administration's foreign policy of increasing trade and cooperation with friendly nations in an effort to prevent war. Roosevelt preferred no legislation to the impartial embargo Congress proposed and worked behind the scenes to modify the proposed neutrality bill.[6]

Moreover, Roosevelt saw international relations and America's role in the world differently than his congressional opponents. Given the realities of modern weapons, the president did not believe that the two oceans were secure barriers or that a policy based only on hemispheric defense would protect American interests. The United States was a world power with global interests that had to be defended. Roosevelt saw American peace and prosperity as dependent upon developments outside the Western Hemisphere. An interdependent world meant cooperation with other nations, collective security for defense, and alliances when necessary to protect legitimate interests and American values in the world. Thus, the United States had to play an active role internationally to defend these interests and protect its institutions and way of life in a world threatened by militaristic dictators.

Yet, by the summer of 1935 it was clear that the neutrality legislation would pass and any direct opposition by the president would lead to a political defeat, possibly derail his domestic legislation, and harm his chances at reelection in 1936. Congress, seeking to prevent the United States from fighting World War I again, established a rigid neutrality law and an impartial arms embargo. It appeared, as Senator Hiram Johnson declared, that the passage of the Neutrality Act of 1935 marked the "triumph of the so-called isolationists and . . . the downfall, although we may not know it, of the internationalist."[7]

The final constraint on making foreign policy was the ambivalent response in the United States to the rise of Hitler to power in Germany and Japan's aggression against China. On the one hand, the American public and U.S. policymakers had no great enthusiasm for the Nazi Party or Hitler. The Nazis' employed unsavory and antidemocratic tactics, and Hitler threatened to undo the Versailles Treaty and upset the political stability in Europe. On the other hand, the United States had developed a favorable analysis and understanding of fascism in Italy, where Benito Mussolini's seizure of power was seen as providing stability, conditions conducive for American trade and business, and a force against the spread of communism. American leaders, believing the key was to support the "moderate" fascists against the "extremist" elements, had easily accommodated their policy to Mussolini's fascist regime and for over a decade had cooperated with Rome on a number of issues.[8] This experience provided the initial basis for policy toward Nazi Germany.

In addition, prior to 1938 no senior policymakers advocated a policy of confrontation with Germany. The last war had brought instability, the decline of the old order, and revolution in its wake; and there was reason to believe the same would occur if war again broke out in Europe. Hemmed in by public opinion and congressional legislation, focused primarily on domestic recovery, and guided by his goals of preventing war, fostering greater international trade and cooperation, and isolating the political left in Europe, Roosevelt sought to redress what were seen as legitimate grievances by Germany in order to reintegrate it through increased trade into an international order compatible to the United States. Concerning Japan, Roosevelt stood by the Stimson Doctrine and sought ways to protect China and deter Japan from further aggression without causing direct conflict with Tokyo.

Initial Policies

The priority of domestic needs over foreign policy at the outset of the Roosevelt administration was clearly demonstrated in the president's first international act. The London Economic Conference, which the United States via the Hoover administration agreed to participate in, met in June 1933 to discuss trade and arms reduction. Prior to the meeting, the president had decided to take the dollar off the gold standard so he could raise the prices on U.S. goods and engage in deficit spending to finance public works projects and spur the economy. While Roosevelt sent Hull as the head of the U.S. delegation, he did so without providing any instructions and with little confidence that much good would be accomplished. The conference got off to a poor start when British prime minister Ramsey MacDonald, in his opening remarks, brought up war debts, which it had been agreed would not be a subject of the meetings. From Roosevelt's point of view, the conference went from bad to worse when the delegates began discussing a new international monetary system to stabilize currencies that would fix the value of the dollar to a set standard. The president cabled Hull that he "would find it as a catastrophe amounting to a world tragedy" if the conference allowed itself "to be diverted by the proposal of a purely artificial and temporary experiment" related to the monetary exchanges of a few nations. Roosevelt refused to accept any international agreement that would "erect probable barriers against our own economic fiscal development."[9] The emergency at home was the priority, and the president was not going to allow the New Deal to be limited in what it could try by an agreement that held no promise for increasing international commerce or improving economic conditions in the world. The president's so-called bombshell message ensured the failure of the meeting in London.

Roosevelt's other significant foreign policy action in 1933 was the recognition of the Soviet Union. The policy of nonrecognition of the Soviet Union was based on the Bolsheviks repudiation of the czars' debts, revolutionary activity abroad, and failure to uphold international agreements. The president, however, could see no reason to continue to ignore the Soviet Union and hoped that recognition might increase trade while helping to provide a deterrent against Japan. Little came of this on either front, and Roosevelt did not make improving relations with the Soviet Union a priority, in part because his step was met with hostility in the State Department, which remained rabidly anti-Soviet throughout the 1930s. Robert Kelley's Division of Eastern European Affairs continually found the communist menace at Europe's doorstep and worked hard to make the containment of bolshevism and suspicions of the Soviet Union main features of American diplomacy. This made the United States skeptical of any diplomatic proposals or suggestions that came from Moscow as it firmly believed that the Soviet Union could not be trusted. Soviet dictator Joseph Stalin's brutal collectivization of agriculture and purges confirmed these negative views. For most of the decade, therefore, the Soviet Union was held at arm's length, and its efforts at promoting collective security were rebuffed, as fear of the Left dominated American concerns down to 1938.

Roosevelt, when he finally began to give some sustained thought to foreign affairs, turned to increasing international trade through the Reciprocal Trade Act of 1934 as a means to ease the economic crisis at home and promote stability and peace abroad. The president's thinking was guided by his understanding that only by finding markets abroad could the United States maintain prosperity and full employment. During the 1932 presidential campaign, Roosevelt noted that since the closing of the frontier at the end of the nineteenth century, the United States had produced more than could be consumed at home. "Our industrial plant is built," Roosevelt explained, and the "problem just now is whether under existing conditions it is not overbuilt. Our last frontier has long since been reached." The same was true of the overproduction of agricultural products. The "mature economy" thesis that the president expounded demanded more balance in the economy and the better "administrating [of] resources and plants already in hand, of seeking to reestablish foreign markets for our surplus production . . . [and] distributing wealth and products more equitably" if the nation was to return to prosperity.[10] Adjustments of tariffs and improved international trade arrangements were seen as crucial to both prosperity and peace.

The Reciprocal Trade Act allowed the president to negotiate with other nations new agreements that would lower the tariff by up to 50 percent if that country reciprocated by opening up its market to U.S. goods. These new treaties did not need congressional approval and could be renewed beyond their original three-year length. Moreover, the most-favored-nation status was extended automatically to other nations that signed similar agreements with the United States. In theory, this would reduce tariffs not just in bilateral trading, but all around the world. While never the panacea that Hull envisioned, American exports did rise by more than $1 billion over the next five years and the desire to use economic arrangements to solve political problems remained central to the administration's approach to foreign policy.

The Good Neighbor Policy

Since his time in the Wilson administration, Franklin Roosevelt had changed his position and desired to see an end to American military intervention in Latin America. During the 1920s he had taken the position that the "single-handed intervention by us in the internal affairs of other nations must end; with the cooperation of others we shall have more order in this Hemisphere and less dislike."[11] In the only specific foreign policy proposal in his inauguration speech, Roosevelt announced a new direction for U.S. policy toward Latin America, a policy of the "good neighbor . . . who resolutely respects himself and, because he does so, respects the rights of others."[12] Looking to improve relations with Latin America to increase trade, aid economic recovery at home, and forestall unrest, the Good Neighbor policy, formally set out on December 28, 1933, renounced unilateral U.S. intervention.

In developing his policy, Roosevelt relied on the advice of Sumner Welles. An old friend of the president's, Welles oversaw the policy, first as ambassador to Cuba and then as undersecretary of state. Welles had experience in the State Department working in Latin America and, having written a two-volume study of the Dominican Republic during the 1920s, was considered a leading expert on the region. Similar to Roosevelt, he opposed continued U.S. intervention in the Caribbean because it created instability rather than order. For both men, some other form of political stability beyond American forces was necessary to eliminate the problems of the area before revolts broke out. Stability, they believed, would allow for economic growth that would benefit both the Latin American nations and the United States. The Good Neighbor policy was based on treating Latin American countries as sovereign, independent states and preventing the rise of the conditions that produced revolutions. While the policy rejected military intervention, it did not mean an end to American influence or efforts to shape events in Latin America.

The new policy was quickly tested in Cuba, where unrest grew throughout 1933. Since 1903, when the Platt Amendment was adopted, the United States had intervened consistently at such moments, sending troops to Cuba four different times over the previous three decades. Events in Havana appeared to invite a fifth round of intervention by American forces to quell the unrest, protect American investments and property, and ensure American control of the key sea-lanes to the Panama Canal through its naval base at Guantanimo. Between August 1933, when the dictator Gerald Machado lost power, and January 1934, when Fulgencio Batista installed a government with Washington's support, Cuba had five different presidents in as many months. Having announced the Good Neighbor policy, Roosevelt could not resort to a military mission and searched for a local leader who could establish order and prevent any radical challenges to substantial American interests in Cuba.

The collapse of the world economy hit Latin America hard as the price for its raw materials and agricultural products plummeted. In Cuba, the drastic drop in the price of sugar brought an economic collapse to the island, political unrest, and demands for reform and Machado's ouster. When Welles arrived in Havana, he had to find a way to restore stability without resorting to the threat of American intervention. His initial approach to the problem was to negotiate a new trade agreement between the United States and Cuba on the assumption that an economic revival would bring political stability, quiet the unrest, and serve as a model for the Good Neighbor policy and relations with other nations in the hemisphere. After a week in Cuba, Welles was optimistic that an early economic agreement that would stabilize Cuba and protect American interests could be reached.

Welles, however, underestimated the extent of opposition to Machado's continued rule and found it impossible to stem the tide demanding the dictator's removal. The ambassador pressured Machado to carry out reforms, but this just aided the opposition and furthered the political stalemate that developed. By summer, Welles decided that Machado had to be removed but faced the problem of how to do this without it appearing as just another case of American intervention.

On August 4, a general strike spread across Cuba and effectively brought an end to Machado's rule. Welles informed Machado that to salvage the situation short of a revolution he would have to resign. The new government of Carlos Manuel de Cespedes provided no resolution to the problems as he lacked support from important groups. After less than a month in office, Cespedes was overthrown in September by the "Sergeants Revolution," which installed Professor Ramón Grau San Martín, a leading reformer. Grau, using the slogan "Cuba for Cubans," promised to unilaterally eliminate the Platt Amendment, suspend payments on loans to the United States, and nationalize parts of the sugar industry.

Having lost control of the situation, Welles now sought pressure from Washington to oust Grau from power. The ambassador saw Grau as an irresponsible leader surrounded by people who held communist ideas and sought to harm American interests on the island. Reports of communist activities became daily components of Welles's reporting, and he requested that the president withhold recognition of the Grau government and send American troops to restore Cespedes to power and protect American interests. Roosevelt and Hull agreed to nonrecognition but stopped short of sending troops. Instead, economic pressure was applied and twelve ships were dispatched to the Cuban coast to reassure Americans there and to intimidate the government. For his part, Welles turned to Batista, a sergeant in the army, and encouraged him to oust Grau and restore good relations with the United States.

The economic weapon had the impact Welles sought as Grau could not provide any relief from the economic crisis and opponents of the government gained strength. On January 13, 1934, Batista deposed Grau and two days later established Carlos Mendieta as president of Cuba. The United States rewarded Batista by quickly recognizing this government, agreeing to abandon the Platt Amendment, and signing a new commercial treaty with Cuba that increased its sugar quota and extended loans to the island. Reviewing Cuba's recent history, the State Department had no doubt that Batista had saved the nation from disorder and anarchy. The embassy in Havana reported that "communism appear[ed] to be concentrating its efforts on Cuba" and was aided by Grau who made "little effort . . . to control communist agitation and none to suppress it."[13] Thus Batista was seen as invaluable for Cuba because in Washington's eyes he had saved it from bolshevism and in doing so had protected American interests.

The Roosevelt administration turned to strongmen to impose order in other nations, such as Nicaragua, El Salvador, and the Dominican Republic, as a replacement for intervention. Support for right-wing dictatorships became a critical component of U.S. policy as it was believed that the people of Latin America were incapable of democratic government. Authoritarian rulers, American leaders believed, would provide stability in nations unprepared for self-rule, protect American interests, and prevent the spread of communism.

There was more, however, to the Good Neighbor policy than just stability. The administration sought to create greater hemispheric unity through reciprocal trade agreements to increase trade and prosperity and to gain protection for American investments and interests in the region. In pursuit of this goal, Washington was able to sign new trade agreements with eleven Latin American nations by the end of the decade. These trade treaties were also seen as essential for greater cooperation on other issues, such as Pan-American cooperation and security.

In a series of Inter-American conferences, the United States promoted the idea of hemisphere solidarity in the face of the growing crises in Europe and Asia. Demonstrating the significance attached to these efforts, at the Inter-American Conference for the Maintenance of Peace in December 1936, President Roosevelt was present for the opening ceremonies and Secretary of State Hull led the U.S. delegation. Among the agreements reached were a protocol on nonintervention and an agreement for all nations to consult in the event of war, either in the hemisphere or outside of it. In 1938, this was expanded to allow any nation to call for consultation if there was a threat to the hemisphere. Whatever shortcomings the Good Neighbor policy had, it led to an improvement of relations as most people in Latin America welcomed it.

After war broke out in Europe in 1939, the United States joined the other twenty-one republics in issuing a declaration of neutrality and proclaiming a 300-mile wide security zone around North and South America. The next year, after the fall of France, Belgium, Holland, and Luxembourg, all the nations of the Americas agreed to a policy that opposed the transfer of a remaining European colony from one nation to another and a "Declaration of Reciprocal Assistance" that declared any attack on one state an act of aggression against all nations. This new Pan-American spirit was vital during the war as it allowed the United States the use of bases for military operations and provided access to critical raw materials for the war effort. In all, the United States signed base agreements with sixteen nations. This plan for hemispheric defense met no opposition at home and provided Roosevelt with a starting point to define American security needs and meet the challenges posed by Germany and Japan later in the decade. Thus, thanks to the Good Neighbor policy, when World War II broke out, the system of obtaining cooperation, bases, and crucial minerals from Latin America was already in place.

Challenge in East Asia

Turning to East Asia, Roosevelt was unsure how best to contain Japan's aggression. Roosevelt, as he had promised Stimson, maintained the policy of nonrecognition of Japan's conquest of Manchuria, but it was not clear what actions beyond the Stimson Doctrine could be taken. The administration sought to promote trade with both China and Japan while it protected China from any further territorial losses and took some steps to signal Tokyo that it disapproved of its actions toward China. Still, trade with Japan was three times greater than that with China, and economic sanctions would hurt the United States at a time when it was searching for all the markets it could find and only encourage Japan to seek unilateral solutions to its economic problems through expansion. In addition, in attempting to construct a policy to deter Japan and protect American interests in the region, the administration acknowledged China's failings in effectively controlling its territory and stabilizing its rule. Chiang Kai-shek's government did not have broad-based support, was marred by corruption on all levels, lacked the organization and leadership necessary to address China's problems, and was unable to protect its borders. The result was a fragmented nation with warlords still ruling parts of the south and west, a growing communist movement, and Japan's taking of Manchuria.

While the United States did not believe Japan required urgent opposition, it clearly understood Japan's ability to challenge American interests and policies and become an enemy of the United States in East Asia and the Pacific. The extent of the problem was set out by American ambassador to Japan Joseph Grew in a May 1933 analysis that Hull forward to Roosevelt. Grew sought to make clear Japan's military potential and argued that it would be wrong for the United States to underestimate Japan's strength. Japan was, he noted, often seen "as a small, overcrowded nation . . . without natural resources, and largely dependent upon foreign sources for its food-stuffs." With the taking of Manchuria, Japan's empire was larger than the combined territories of Belgium, Denmark, France, Germany, the Nether-lands, Spain, and Switzerland, and controlled over 120 million people, al-most equal to the U.S. population. Moreover, the Japanese "are intelligent, industrious, energetic, extremely nationalistic, war-loving, aggressive and, it must be admitted, somewhat unscrupulous." Japan could feed its entire people and had "developed its industries in recent years until it is able to supply itself with all of the necessities of life, and can build all the ships, and make all the airplanes, tanks, guns, ammunition, chemicals, etc., needed to wage a severe war, if it is not too protracted." All of this supported the most "powerful fighting machine in the world today" that "is designed for the purpose of keeping Western nations from interfering while Japan car-ries out its ambitions in Asia."[14]

Japanese leaders, Grew opined, saw Tokyo's control over East Asia as "the nation's natural expansion," something akin to America's own sense of Manifest Destiny. What made all this most dangerous was "the national morale and espirit de corps—a spirit which perhaps has not been equaled since the days when the Mongol hordes followed Genghis Khan in his con-quest of Asia." Grew concluded by noting that the strength of a nation driven by "great moral determination, fired with national ambition, and peopled by a race with unbounded capacity for courageous self-sacrifice is not easy to overestimate."[15]

Acknowledging this problem, Roosevelt sought ways to put pressure on Japan and to aid China. In 1933, Congress granted his request for a $50 million credit for China to purchase agricultural products and airplane parts in the United States. In addition, the president authorized the construction of thirty new warships and two aircraft carriers to bring the United States closer to full capacity under the Washington Treaty as the first step toward meeting Japan's growing threat. The administration also pressed Japan on renewing the naval treaty restrictions, which would end in 1936 if one of the signatory nations renounced its provisions by December 1934. Roosevelt was determined that if the limits on navies ended the responsibility would be clearly Tokyo's. When Japan did disavow the treaty, Roosevelt was able to obtain in early 1936 a significant increase in naval spending to begin modernizing the American fleet.

The differences between Washington and Tokyo were made clear in April 1934 during the so-called Amau incident. Foreign Office spokesman Amau Eiji announced that Japan alone had the right to preserve the peace and order in East Asia, most notably in China, and that any further military aid or other efforts to supply China would be viewed as hostile actions toward Japan. In making this statement, Tokyo renounced all international agreements related to China, most notably the Open Door, and established China as a protectorate of Japan under what would become the Greater East Asian Co-Prosperity Sphere.

The United States rejected this position and reiterated its support for the Open Door policy and the need for nations to respect the rights of others and adhere to international agreements. As the Far Eastern Division of the State Department noted in a thirty-eight-page analysis of the problems in relations with Japan in April 1934, Japan was seeking U.S. and British surrender of their interests in East Asia and the recognition of "Japan's 'Monroe Doctrine for Asia'" in preparation for further action against China. The Japanese sought to "promote and facilitate the attainment by Japan of a paramount and dominating position in the Far East," and the U.S. response had to be adherence to existing agreements and not favoring any country in the region or accepting a policy that provides "the advantage or disadvantage of any."[16]

In May, Japan's ambassador to the United States, Hirosi Saito, met with Cordell Hull to officially present Japan's position. On May 16, the ambassador told Hull that in Japan it was believed "that the United States in the past had sought to checkmate his country in most all of its plans, ideas or moves in the way of progress externally." In the prepared memorandum that he handed to Hull, Saito requested that the United States recognize Japan's sphere of influence in China in return for Japan's respect for the Monroe Doctrine. The western Pacific "lies within [Japan's] proper and legitimate power to establish a reign of law and order" as the main stabilizing power.[17]

The two men met again three days later to discuss the note and the American response. Saito agreed that the main point was that "his Government did feel that it had a special interest in preserving peace and order in

China." Hull responded by setting out the fundamental assumptions behind the Open Door policy, telling the ambassador that it would be "more profitable" for Japan to work cooperatively to "retain the perfect understanding and the friendship of all civilized nations" to promote the "welfare of their respective peoples and at the same time meet their duties to civilization and to the more backward populations of the world." The concern was that Japan was seeking an empire and not just a protection of its rights and stability in the region, which could best be obtained through international agreements. Given the current world crisis, it was crucial that "civilized countries should be especially vigilant to observe and to preserve both legal and moral obligations" and that nations "work whole-heartedly together; and that this action of course would, more fully than any other, promote the welfare of the people of each and also best preserve civilization."[18] This exchange made it clear that the two nations were talking past each other and that it would be difficult to find a common ground for a resolution or a compromise.

Japan's withdrawal from the League of Nations in March 1933 and abrogation of the naval treaty at the end of 1934 confirmed American concerns that Tokyo was embarking on a course of expansion that would collide with American interests in East Asia. Stanley Hornbeck, the head of the Far Eastern Division of the State Department, noted that it was now "a fact that the Japanese conceptions today of legality, of morality and of expediency differ from ours."[19] In early 1935, Ambassador Grew provided Hull a two-part analysis of Japan's decisions that the secretary of state forwarded to President Roosevelt. Given the prospect of an enlarged Japanese navy, Grew urged that the United States "be adequately prepared to meet all eventualities in the Far East." It was "the general conclusion . . . that there exists in Japan today a definite urge toward economic and political expansion in East Asia and, as a corollary, a growing pressure against the interests of western nations, including the interests of the United States." What Grew termed "the present-day chauvinism in Japan" stemmed from a resentment of the West and a sense of being accorded second-class status in international relations. Tokyo believed that Japan occupied "a position which entitles them to the same consideration in the Far East that the British and the French claim in the affairs of Europe or even the United States in the Western Hemisphere, and they intend to assert and maintain this position with all the strength at their command."[20]

Internal factors—notably overpopulation, lack of natural resources, industrialization, and the desire to increase the standard of living on the home islands—drove Japanese expansion. "With a larger sphere of activity Japanese industry and commerce will expand further and remove the spectre of restricted markets." It was Tokyo's position that "if this has to be done at others' expense it cannot be helped." All of this was part of Japan's sense of "manifest destiny" to dominate and protect East Asia and need for a safety valve for its population. Thus, it was essential to see Japan's actions, Grew noted, "as the reasonable and logical operation of well-nigh irrepressible forces based on the underlying principle of self preservation."[21]

Grew recommended that the U.S. response be based on two concurrent principles. First, the United States needed a policy of "national preparedness for the purpose of protecting our legitimate interests in the Far East." Second, the ambassador suggested "a sympathetic, co-operative and helpful attitude toward Japan."[22] Grew's ambivalence reflected overall American policy. The Roosevelt administration worried about Japan's actions, but up to this point no significant U.S. material interest had been harmed. Yet, no action would send the wrong signal that Washington was acquiescing to Tokyo's claims and maneuvers. Still, it was not clear what steps could or should be taken to deter Japan's expansion.

Given this, the administration continued to make its opposition to Japan's emerging policy known to Tokyo and sent aid to China even though that only served to further antagonize Japan and had little impact given the disarray of the Chinese government and its inability to resist Japan's actions. But what other options were there, administration officials asked? Certainly, no one was proposing going to war, alone or with other nations, over China in the middle of the 1930s, and Roosevelt was not willing to concede the Open Door policy to Japan's version of a sphere of influence. The president, therefore, sought to provide whatever aid he could to China while he continued to make Tokyo aware of American opposition to further expansion and to build up American naval power in the hopes of deterring Japan's plan of dominating East Asia.

Crisis in Europe

The outbreak of the Italo-Ethiopian War in October 1935 forced President Roosevelt to give more attention to the building international crisis in Europe. When Italy invaded Ethiopia on October 3, Roosevelt reacted angrily; he immediately instructed Secretary of State Hull to invoke the recently passed Neutrality Act to deny Italy access to American arms and warned

American traders that they conducted business with Italy at their own risk. Hull added a call for a "moral embargo" by American companies on the shipment of war-related items, such as oil, copper, and steel. The administration would not, however, impose a complete embargo, that is, one enforced by the government, which would antagonize Benito Mussolini and hurt his war effort. Washington feared that restrictions by the West on Rome might bring about a conflict over resources between Italy and Great Britain in the Mediterranean and possibly lead to a European war.

It was not Italian domination of Ethiopia but the danger of the conflict spreading that concerned the White House. Little was done to aid Ethiopia, and certainly the United States did not intend to adopt an anticolonial policy at this time. Roosevelt saw the war as a misguided adventure by Italy, and not as naked aggression that threatened the world's general peace and stability, for little gain. In the words of Undersecretary of State William Phillips, the State Department saw "Mussolini's 'enterprise' as a detail" that had to be kept in perspective. "Germany remained the key to the whole European situation."[23]

Prior to the war, the president had written to his ambassador in Italy, Breckinridge Long, "These are without doubt the most hair trigger times the world has gone through in your life time or mine. I do not even exclude June and July, 1914, because at that time there was economic and social stability, with only the loom of war by Governments in accordance with preconceived ideas and prognostications. Today there is not one element alone but three or more."[24] While Roosevelt did not elaborate on what these elements were in his letter, his speeches and writings the rest of the year and the next demonstrate that the president was worried that with the lack of economic and political stability in Europe and the growing strength of the Left caused by the Great Depression, the impact of another war and its aftermath would prove to be devastating and even more revolutionary than that following the Great War. Just prior to the outbreak of fighting in Africa, Roosevelt spoke to the nation about the danger of foreign wars "at this moment to the future of civilization." He referred to World War I as the "folly of twenty years ago" and argued that the current danger in Europe was even greater. A repeat would "drag civilization to a level from which world wide recovery may be all but impossible."[25]

The Italian invasion of Ethiopia prompted Roosevelt to deliver a major foreign policy speech on Armistice Day 1935. The president again sounded the theme of fear about the consequences of war during such unstable times. People had to come to understand that the "elation and prosperity which may come from a new war must lead—for those who survive it—to economic and social collapse more sweeping than anywhere experienced in the past."[26] Early the next year, Roosevelt wrote, "One cannot help feeling that the whole European panorama is fundamentally blacker than any time," and he compared the potential for revolutionary upheaval to that of 1848 and 1917. He concluded that these "may be the last days of the period of peace before a long chaos."[27]

Events in Spain served to deepen this concern. In July 1936, civil war broke out when Gen. Francisco Franco's fascist rebels attacked the republican Popular Front government in Madrid. While the United States joined with Great Britain and France in declaring neutrality, Germany and Italy aided Franco's forces, and the Soviet Union, following its policy of a united front of progressive forces against fascism, provided material assistance to the Loyalists. American nonintervention stemmed from Washington's fear of the war in Spain spilling over the Pyrenees into a wider European conflagration and the desire to avoid cooperating with the Left in containing the threat of fascism. The Spanish Civil War demonstrated the potential danger of general war and the ideological component Washington feared.

From its founding in 1931, American officials were skeptical of the Spanish Republic and feared that it was just a matter of time before it would go Bolshevik. Because of its weakness and confiscatory policy toward foreign investments, embassy officials in Madrid believed that the new government represented "a Kerensky interlude" preceding a communist takeover.[28] The formation of the Popular Front government of leftist parties in early 1936, modeled on the Soviet Union's idea of a united front, caused relations between the United States and Spain to break down almost completely before the civil war. The State Department saw the Popular Front as nothing more than a cover-up for Soviet aggression and a different means of bringing about communist takeovers of other nations, what Ambassador to the Soviet Union William Bullitt termed the "tactics of the Trojan horse." Undersecretary of State William Phillips saw the popular front strategy as a way of "encouraging communistic efforts in other countries," while Ambassador to Spain Claude Bowers worried that "there are communistic elements in Spain that are working toward another French Revolution with its terror."[29]

The Neutrality Act did not cover a civil war, and there was no legal basis to deny the sale of weapons to the Spanish Republic. Still, given the views of American officials and the fear of strengthening the Left, the United States never would have come to the aid of the Loyalists. Summarizing the State Department's position, Phillips noted, "If the government wins . . . communism throughout Europe will be immensely stimulated."[30] Having defined the civil war as a revolt against a communist government, and not the spread of fascism, the solution was to deny arms to the Loyalists. A "moral embargo" on all weapons sales to the Spanish Republic was implemented, and neutrality became policy.

Even German and Italian aid to Franco was interpreted in the best light possible, as defensive actions against the spread of communism. Phillips believed that both nations were "forced to concern [themselves] with the Spanish situation because of the original actions of Soviet Russia in seeking to communize Spain with the consequent menace to established systems in neighboring countries." From Berlin, Ambassador William Dodd, a harsh critic of Hitler's regime, wrote that in considering aid to Franco, "regard should be paid to the . . . antipathy of Hitler and Mussolini toward the establishment of a 'Red' Government in Spain which unquestionably is a motivating factor in their Spanish policy." The Western European branch of the State Department concurred and noted that Germany and Italy "considered that Russia had intervened in Spain and that they were merely acting defensively." The primary objective was to stop communism in Spain.[31]

Many in the United States opposed this policy, and several thousand eventually defied the government and went to Spain to fight the spread of fascism. Only after Germany's taking of Austria in 1938 and the conclusion that appeasement was failing did most Americans come to see the Spanish Civil War as part of a larger fascist threat and the policy as a mistake. President Roosevelt reached the same conclusion and in 1939, too late to help the Loyalist cause, changed American policy to allow for the sale of supplies to Spain.

With tensions mounting in Europe, warfare breaking out on its periphery, and Japan becoming more aggressive, Roosevelt knew that some action was necessary if peace was to be maintained and a general war averted. The president feared another war for good reason; he had witnessed the death and destruction of World War I and the upheavals it was still bringing to the world. He did not, however, want foreign policy to become an issue in his reelection campaign, and he offered no new plans or ideas on international affairs. If Roosevelt had decided to use the campaign to address the building crises in Europe and Asia, his choices of how to approach the issue would have been limited. The president could have sided with the isolationists' sentiment, maintained strict neutrality, strengthened hemispheric defense, and steered clear of Europe's problems. While a popular position, Roosevelt saw this as shortsighted to America's interests and security, an abandonment of his internationalist beliefs, and an abdication by the United States of its responsibility as a great nation.

Another option open to the president was to embrace the Soviet Union's call for a united front against fascism and to attempt to forge a coalition to oppose Germany. This was rejected out of hand for two reasons. First, it was a political impossibility as such a policy would receive no support. Second, it was contrary to what Roosevelt was trying to accomplish, the avoidance of war. A popular front against fascism, Roosevelt was sure, would lead to a conflict that would bring massive destruction, social upheaval, and revolution to Europe. This was exactly what the president was trying to prevent. The question for Roosevelt was how to modify or contain Germany and deter Japan without relying on the Soviet Union and augmenting the influence of the European left, and without going to war.

In this context the president decided in 1937 on a third option: negotiate with Germany to address crucial economic issues while seeking to improve relations with Great Britain and setting out to educate the American public about the dangers the United States faced abroad. This built on traditional American policies of the Monroe Doctrine and hemispheric defense, international trade, the rights of neutrals, and the Open Door and simultaneously began to expand the meaning of what was necessary for the nation's defense and shifted the nation's policy away from neutrality toward cooperation with allies and collective security. In doing so, the president began his long campaign to overcome noninterventionist sentiment in America.

CHAPTER 3

THE TURN TOWARD
INTERNATIONALISM

THE EVENTS OF 1936 BEGAN EUROPE'S DESCENT INTO WAR. In March, German forces reoccupied the demilitarized Rhineland. In May, Italy completed its conquest of Ethiopia, and in July, the Spanish Civil War began. The mounting tensions in Europe and Japan's attack on China in July 1937 leading to full-scale war in Asia led President Roosevelt, with his reelection safely behind him, to search for a policy to promote peace and protect American interests. In late 1937, the president decided to pursue economic appeasement toward Germany while he simultaneously set out to educate the American people about the dangers the United States faced abroad. The effort to redirect public opinion was designed to gain support for an internationalist foreign policy based on deterrence, preparedness, and close relations with Great Britain. The president sought to make the American public aware that its security depended as much on developments on the other sides of the two oceans as it did on securing the Western Hemisphere.

In making the case for an internationalist approach to foreign affairs, Roosevelt and his supporters argued that as a great power the United States had a vital interest in world affairs, that developments overseas were essential to its national security and prosperity, that it was important to protect both the valid and peaceful interests of the nation and its values and institutions abroad, and that American security was now being threatened by the actions of Germany and Japan. Given this, it was essential that the nation become more involved in world affairs and that it prepare to defend itself in case Roosevelt's negotiations did not preserve the peace. In sum, the president argued that Germany and Japan not only threatened America's legitimate interests abroad and national security at home but also represented the antithesis of American values. The rulers in Berlin and Tokyo had destroyed freedom in their own nations and were embarked upon a course of expansion that threatened freedom and liberty in other parts of the world, including the Western Hemisphere and the United States, as they trampled on treaties and international law and showed no signs of restraint in pursuing their objectives of total power and domination.

The problems in Europe were seen as the greatest danger to the United States, but it was in the wake of the Japanese attack on China that Roosevelt first fully outlined his thoughts on the mounting crises. In his October 1937 Quarantine Speech, the president set out his understanding of the U.S. place in the world, the challenges America confronted, and the basis for what would develop into his version of a just war doctrine. While his efforts in 1937–1939 failed to prevent war, they did begin the process of creating a close tie with Great Britain, increasing American preparedness for fighting, and shifting public opinion away from neutrality toward the internationalist position the president more and more forcefully advocated.

Climate of Opinion

In taking his first steps to confront the challenges posed by Nazi Germany and Imperial Japan, Roosevelt faced an American public that remained decidedly in support of neutrality and wary of any actions by the United States that would involve it in the building crises overseas. In January 1937, a Gallup poll showed that almost 70 percent of the American people supported mandatory neutrality legislation and that 94 percent saw keeping the nation out of war as more important than using U.S. influence to prevent an outbreak of war overseas. In this environment Roosevelt sought to amend the neutrality laws to provide for a cash-and-carry provision and discretionary power for the president in implementing the Neutrality Act.

The idea for cash-and-carry was first proposed by the financier Bernard Baruch, an ardent supporter of Roosevelt and the New Deal. As he explained it in the June 1936 issue of *Current History*, Baruch envisioned a policy that would allow the United States to sell goods to any belligerents, but the terms would be "cash on the barrel-head and come and get it."[1] The appeal of Baruch's proposal was that American producers could sell their goods, while the United States avoided the problems of protecting neutral shipping rights and maintained its neutrality. When the Neutrality Act came up for renewal in early 1937, cash-and-carry was at the center of the debate.

The administration lobbied hard for the adoption of the cash-and-carry amendment along with the provision that the president be granted the authority to decide when to invoke the neutrality laws. Staunch isolationists wanted to maintain mandatory restrictions on the sale of arms to keep the United States free of any involvement in foreign wars. With proponents of cash-and-carry pointing out that the nation would benefit economically while still preserving its neutrality, the die-hard isolationists yielded on allowing the sale of goods but still sought mandatory restrictions. As supporters of discretionary power noted, cash-and-carry would work fine in Europe because Great Britain could get to U.S. ports and secure goods, but it was a problem in Asia because Japan and not China, whose ports were blocked by the Japanese navy, would be able to purchase supplies. Granting the president the discretionary authority to decide when to impose the law would provide greater flexibility and prevent the sale of goods to nations hostile to American interests. In April, Congress passed the revised Neutrality Act with the cash-and-carry provision in place for the next two years. Roosevelt saw this new law as a means to increase American

Roosevelt delivers his famous "Quarantine Speech" in Chicago, October 5, 1937.
Franklin D. Roosevelt Library

influence abroad, promote cooperation with Great Britain, and implement a plan of economic appeasement toward Germany while remaining within the parameters of public opinion.

Economic Appeasement

The policy of economic appeasement was designed to meet Germany's economic needs by providing the country relief from the restrictions of the Versailles Treaty, while opposing territorial expansion to maintain the peace in Europe. It is important to remember that American use of the term "appeasement" was shorthand for calling for negotiations and compromise and that the term did not yet have the negative connotations of a sell-out it received after the 1938 Munich agreement. Economic arrangements were both politically possible, at home and abroad, and seen as the way to secure greater international trade and prevent the feared alternative of a war that would lead to chaos and revolution. American officials fully appreciated the threat Germany posed and sought to address that danger and preserve American interests while avoiding any direct political commitments to Europe that would stir up political opposition at home. This strategy fit well with the Reciprocal Trade Agreement program. Employing Hull's analysis that economic rivalry was the cause of war and that greater international trade would create interdependence, it was believed that once its trade began to improve, Germany would see that its interests were served better through cooperation with the Western democracies than in combating them.

It was also true that the choices of how to approach Europe were limited. The president could side with the isolationists, maintain strict neutrality, strengthen hemispheric defense, steer clear of Europe's problems, and let Europeans worry about the outcome. Adopting this stance certainly would have been in line with public opinion. Roosevelt, however, saw this thinking as the product of a naïve understanding of the realities of the world and American interests, modern warfare, and what was necessary to defend the nation. Moreover, he believed it was an abdication of America's responsibility as a great nation and an abandonment of America's values in the world. The question for Roosevelt was, how could the United States modify or contain Germany without confrontation or relying on the Soviet Union and augmenting the influence of the European left, both of which would bring war? This should not be interpreted as a policy designed to drive Germany to the east to fight the Soviet Union. The United States did not want war anywhere in Europe because the fighting would inevitably spread to the rest of the continent, further destabilizing existing institutions and providing a spark for revolution. Rather, it was to end the need for any German expansion and prevent a disastrous war in Europe.

America's appeasement policy was based on three key assumptions. First, it was the accepted view in Washington that Hitler's rise to power was the result of Germany's harsh treatment under the Treaty of Versailles combined with the economic problems brought on by the Great Depression. Thus, Germany had legitimate grievances that needed to be redressed. Second, the unrest and instability caused by the Great Depression led to a rise of the Left and a need for stability and political order to block communism. A resolution of the economic problems Germany faced, therefore, would lead to political solutions.

Finally, the State Department believed that a split between moderate and extreme fascists defined the Nazi Party. Moderates, it was thought, favored international cooperation and the gradual return to liberal policies once the political and economic crises presented by the threat of communism and unjust agreements were settled. Extremists believed in autarchic, nationalistic economic policies and expansion as the solution to their nation's problems. It was, therefore, seen as essential that Washington develop policies that aided the moderates and isolated the extremists. As the American embassy in Berlin reported, "There is no doubt that a very definite struggle is going on between the violent radical wing of the Nazi Party . . . and what might be termed the more moderate section of the party, headed by Hitler himself . . . which appeal[s] to all civilized and reasonable people."[2] Employing this paradigm, American leaders did not exhibit great concerns about Hitler's initial policies. The Third Reich's decision to free itself of the Treaty of Versailles by leaving the League of Nations was met with understanding in Washington. The German announcement of its plans to rearm in 1934 was accepted without protest as a legitimate action of a nation and not necessarily a sign of future aggression.

In February 1937, the State Department developed its most comprehensive analysis of German fascism, the problems it created for U.S. policy, and how to best approach Berlin to maintain peace in Europe. Contrary to the prevailing wisdom on bolshevism and the Soviet Union, the department found fascism as a system compatible with free trade and liberal governments. Means, therefore, could be developed to convince Germany to reject territorial expansion and economic self-sufficiency for international cooperation. The report explained that the rise of fascism stemmed from a threat from the Left brought about by the Great Depression. "When there is suffering, the dissatisfied masses, with the example of the Russian revolution before them, swing to the Left. The rich and middle classes, in self-defense turn to Fascism." Defining fascism as the natural movement by the respectable classes to defend order and property from communism, the department believed that where fascism was in power, "it must succeed or the masses, this time reinforced by the disillusioned middle classes, will again turn to the Left."[3]

The concern for the rest of the world was the threat of German expansion. "Germany," the report noted, was "at the center of the problem of peace and war. If there is to be war, it will probably take the form of a drive by Germany for sources of raw materials." "Far-seeing statesmen [accepted] that Germany . . . should have access to raw materials" and that Berlin's economic demands were not "unreasonable." Washington viewed the adoption of a policy of economic autarky as misguided, and the Nazis could be persuaded to abandon it under the right circumstances. "The immediate objective, then, of an intervention on the part of the United States . . . would be to precipitate the movement for a general political and economic settlement which would obviate the necessity for Germany to strike out to obtain the resources of raw materials in markets deemed by the German leaders necessary to maintain the standard of living of the German people."[4]

As the State Department concluded, "economic appeasement should prove to be the surest route to world peace." Appeasement was essential if war was to be avoided. "If Fascism cannot succeed by persuasion" to solve Germany's problems, "it must succeed by force." The United States, therefore, had to assist German economic recovery. The report bluntly noted that "the problem of European peace . . . may be clearly defined: Can a compromise be found, or a price paid, which will satisfy the economic necessities of the German people, without war . . . ? If so, there will be no war; if no, war is possible, if not probable."[5]

The president knew there were no easy answers and no guarantees. As European nations rearmed themselves, he worried that there might not be enough time for economic arrangements to take hold. Yet, the president wondered, what other options did he have? Neutrality meant drift and the direction was toward war, a conflagration Roosevelt was sure the United States could not avoid. Collective security was impossible politically. Besides, it meant some type of agreement with the Soviet Union, an agreement

Roosevelt and the State Department were not yet ready to entertain, and disarmament was tied to economic recovery. "How do we make progress," the president asked in May 1937, "if England and France say we cannot help Germany and Italy to achieve economic security if they continue to arm and threaten, while simultaneously Germany and Italy say we must continue to arm and threaten because they will not give us economic security?"[6] Thus, the president's thinking kept coming back to economic solutions and the proposal from Undersecretary of State Sumner Welles for an international conference on disarmament and trade.

In a series of speeches, Welles set out the administration's understanding of the central problems facing Europe, the main assumptions of the internationalist position, and the case for economic appeasement through an international conference. At the heart of the problem were the economic dislocations and problems brought about by the Versailles System and the Great Depression. This was driving nations to change the international status quo and creating the danger of another war. As Welles stated, peace was the "uppermost question in the minds of every one of us today." To secure peace, the United States had to acknowledge "that the greater the economic pressure to which a nation is subjected, the more desperate it becomes in its search for markets for its products or goods." The curtailment of trade, lack of raw materials, and unemployment led governments to the "frantic resort . . . without regard for cost, to the rapid increase of armaments through the manufacture of munitions—for the moment as an expedient for reviving industry and to give employment but eventually and infallibly as a means of acquiring, through conquest, that which they failed to obtain through the peaceful channels of normal trade." These conditions called for the U.S. leadership to build on the Reciprocal Trade Agreement program to open up all channels of trade and to make sure that nations did not resort to force as a road to prosperity.[7]

Reflecting the State Department's analysis concerning the development of fascism, Welles argued that the current tensions with Germany were the result of the structural problems besetting the international system and not the result of the ideology of the Nazi government. "The ills from which the world suffers today," Welles stated in July 1937, "revolve primarily about the fundamental fact that the injustices and maladjustments resulting from the Great War have never yet been rectified." He noted that the United States understood that a general settlement of Europe's problems necessitated a revision of the Treaty of Versailles, which had left

Germany with "intolerable moral and material burdens" imposed upon it by the victors. The lessons to be learned were that "peace of a permanent nature cannot be founded on revenge" and that the international order as currently constructed on this basis was doomed to failure. It was unreasonable to expect the Germans to "face a future without hope" and to toil "in order that they may thus offer reparation for the crimes and mistakes, real or alleged, of an earlier generation." People forced into such a position will always take the first opportunity to free themselves from such an order.[8] Thus, a change in the system would alleviate the current tensions and bring a return to peace, stability, and prosperity.

Even with its rejection of the Treaty of Versailles and League of Nations and its position as a neutral nation, the United States was neither without responsibility nor immune from the dangers growing in Europe. Most notably, the 1930 Hawley-Smoot tariff was a significant factor in the current crisis as it curtailed international trade and "contributed to the creation of all those artificial barriers" to trade "which have become the rule rather than the exception during the past 6 years." Welles found the results, if no changes were made, predictable. "Surely," he opined, "it must be by now universally accepted that economic warfare is one of the chief contributing causes to warfare by force of arms." Renewed fighting would further the economic problems of the United States and inevitably drag the nation into the conflagration. It was, therefore, incumbent upon Washington to propose a remedy.[9]

The basis for peace, Welles noted, was already set out in the reciprocal trade program and model for international cooperation established by the Good Neighbor policy. It was axiomatic to Welles that freer trade would bring prosperity to all nations and reduce international conflict. This was, he believed, being demonstrated in the Western Hemisphere, where the United States had renounced intervention and was reaching mutually beneficial trade agreements with the nations of Latin America, all of which served to provide more markets for American producers while they fostered "conditions which will tend to promote international peace." Only the recognition of the source of international conflict and its remedy "can eliminate the danger of war." It was imperative, therefore, that the United States lead the way "in restoring and maintaining unimpaired the channels of healthy world trade . . . in furthering the cause of peace."[10]

While Congress sought to minimize the danger of the United States being drawn into war through neutrality legislation, it could not insulate the nation from the impact of war. "War," Welles stated, "must inevitably bring with it economic collapse, social chaos, and hitherto unparalleled human destruction and suffering." Spain reflected the exact opposite of the cooperation, trade, and trust that the United States was creating in the Western Hemisphere and contained the condition the Roosevelt administration feared would bring general war to Europe. As Welles observed in setting out his peace plan, the civil war in Spain was "a manifestation of the disease from which this world is suffering" that had its roots in the Great War and the failed peace of Versailles. Spain was the "battleground of fundamentally antagonistic dogmas which men have evolved since the outbreak of World War, which have had their genesis in want and misery," and could easily produce a "spark which may light the conflagration of a major international war." It was no secret that the Soviet Union was aiding the Republican forces and Nazi Germany and Fascist Italy the rebels. "It is in that fact," Welles noted, "that the most immediate danger to the peace of the world lies today."[11]

While the United States remained neutral toward Spain, it could still take steps to prevent the outbreak of a general war. Here Welles set out all the key elements of the administration's internationalist position. He proposed a "broad program for world rehabilitation . . . outside of the realm of those political adjustments in which we have no share [to] restore international confidence and lay those foundations of normal and just international relationships which mean peace." The basic principles to be applied were a respect for treaties among nations and the "revitalization of international morals, which means first and foremost the sanctity of the pledged word given between nations"; a reduction of trade restrictions; the limitation of armaments; and international conferences for the free exchange of ideas and negotiation of agreements to implement these goals. Again, Welles held out the Good Neighbor policy as an example of the proper approach and the recent meeting of the representatives of the American republics and their declaration of adherence to the principles set out by Welles as the instruments of peace.[12]

These steps were essential, Welles concluded, because if war broke out in Europe, the neutrality laws would not shield the United States. "No matter how free from involvement we may remain," Welles declared, "we cannot stay clear of its consequences; we cannot avoid the repercussions of its social and economic results upon our national life." For this reason alone, beyond the responsibilities of the United States as a great power and member of the family of nations, the United States had to play its part "in grappling with the disease which afflicts mankind, before it is too late."[13]

The plan Roosevelt adopted consisted of the United States calling a world conference so that nations would agree on how they could all "obtain the right to have access upon equal and effective terms to raw materials and other elements necessary for their economic life." Arrangements would be based on international cooperation over resources and cooperation on trade with the goal of economic interdependence and shared prosperity leading to a reduction of armaments.[14] The president supported the Welles Plan because it stayed within the parameters of acceptable action domestically and was based on the internationalist tenets for foreign policy that he believed in. Moreover, it reflected the understanding of his administration at the time that the moderate fascists remained in control and could be worked with and that economic appeasement of Germany could succeed without assistance from the Soviet Union. Finally, the president feared that a policy that only condemned Hitler's actions without offering a solution to what were perceived as legitimate grievances would drive the Führer into an alliance with Mussolini and bring about war. Some formula was needed to enable Germany to be integrated into the international system short of direct confrontation. Unable to advocate collective security, Roosevelt saw no other way to approach the German problem, and the prevailing interpretation of fascism gave him hope that a solution was possible.

Secretary of State Hull agreed with the president's and Welles's analysis and proposal but insisted that the British first be advised of the plan before Roosevelt took the initiative of extending invitations to the nations of Europe. As presented to the British in January 1938, the aim of the conference was to foster an "understanding between this country and the leading powers of Europe to achieve economic co-operation" to create an "international economy based on reduced armaments, a greater common use of world resources, and the improvement and simplification of economic relations" among nations.[15] British prime minister Neville Chamberlain had been formulating his own appeasement policy based on bilateral negotiations between London and Berlin, piecemeal concessions to Germany, and territorial adjustments in Eastern Europe. Chamberlain, who distrusted the United States and believed that, based on Washington's rejection of the Treaty of Versailles, it could not be counted on to back up any arrangements, rejected Welles's proposal on the grounds that it would interfere with his own negotiations with Berlin. The prime minister informed

Roosevelt that any effort by the United States at that time to call for a world conference would "delay consideration of specific points which must be settled if appeasement is to be achieved."[16]

Roosevelt and Welles were upset by Chamberlain's rejection of the U.S. proposal. American leaders believed that a general settlement of Europe's problems had to be reached to avoid war, while Chamberlain was pursuing a piecemeal approach that did not get to the central problems. In effect, Chamberlain had excluded the United States from participating in any settlement. In February, British foreign minister Anthony Eden persuaded Chamberlain to open discussions with the United States based on the Welles Plan. Hitler's annexation of Austria on March 12, 1938, brought an end to these discussions and to using the Welles Plan as a basis for peace.

In the wake of the *Anschluss*, Chamberlain returned to his negotiations with Berlin. With no other avenues open to him, Roosevelt backed the prime minister's efforts. He released a statement on April 19 endorsing Chamberlain's current discussion and reiterating that the United States "urged the promotion of peace through the finding of means for economic appeasement."[17] Events, however, were moving quickly as Hitler escalated his demands to include the absorption of the Sudetenland in Czechoslovakia into the Third Reich. The basis of the German claim was that the majority of the people in this part of Czechoslovakia spoke German and, therefore, should be part of the German nation. Prague initially resisted Berlin's pressure and sought assistance from other nations against Germany. France and Great Britain were opposed to any actions that would bring war. While the Soviet Union indicated it would use force, Poland and Romania refused to allow its forces to cross their borders. Isolated, in late September, Czechoslovakia yielded to pressure from London and announced it would surrender the territory to Germany.

Roosevelt contacted the British, French, Germans, Italians, and Czechs, to urge them all to continue negotiations and bring a peaceful resolution to the crisis. The State Department supported ceding more territory to Germany, arguing that it was legitimate to bring all German-speaking people into one nation. As Assistant Secretary of State Adolf Berle advised Roosevelt, in responding to the taking of the Sudetenland by Germany, the United States should not let "emotion" obscure its judgment. If it was any other leader but Hitler, the action would be viewed as "undoing the unsound work of Versailles" and a prosperous Germany will not "forever be the hideous picture it is today."[18] After Chamberlain's announcement that he would meet Hitler and Mussolini in Munich to work out an agreement around the transfer of territory, Roosevelt sent him a two-word cable: "Good Man."[19] The State Department believed that the Munich conference provided an opportunity for an overall settlement of Europe's problems and that an "opportunity for real appeasement resting on sound economic foundations was at hand." As Welles told the nation in a radio speech on October 3, the Munich conference created the best opportunity since the Versailles Treaty "for the establishment by the nations of the world of a new world order based upon justice and upon law."[20]

The optimism over the Munich conference was short-lived, however, in the face of Germany's renewed repression of German Jews and continued belligerence. The State Department began what Berle called its "death watch" on Europe. By late October, it was irrevocably clear to the president that appeasement had failed and war was coming. As Roosevelt told Secretary of the Treasury Henry Morganthau, "These trade treaties are just too god-damned slow, the world is marching too fast. They're just too slow."[21] On November 15, he called the American ambassador to Berlin home for consultations, and the ambassador never returned to Germany. Roosevelt concluded that Hitler was a fanatic, "a pure unadulterated devil," who could not recognize Germany's real interests or be reached by rational appeals.[22] The only option now, the president believed, was to accelerate military spending and his efforts to shift American public opinion away from neutrality and in support of internationalism as Hitler would have to be stopped by force. This quest to change the public's understanding of events had begun the previous fall in response to developments in East Asia.

The Quarantine Speech

In July 1937, full-scale fighting erupted in China in the wake of a clash between Japanese and Chinese soldiers at the Marco Polo Bridge. While the initial encounter on July 7 was only a minor skirmish, it was clear by September that Japan intended to use the incident as a pretext for an all-out assault on China and that the talks to arrange a cease-fire were just a smokescreen to hide Tokyo's intention of establishing the Greater East Asian Co-Prosperity Sphere and its hegemony over East Asia. American sympathies were clearly with China, and Japan was labeled the aggressor in all accounts. Still, the supporters of neutrality insisted that the United States keep clear of the fighting and that the president enact the neutrality law. This led to the first direct clash between Roosevelt and the noninterventionists. Roosevelt's dilemma was how to provide aid to China and resist Japan without getting too far ahead of public opinion. As he told Morganthau, it was "a matter of longtime education."[23]

If the president invoked the 1937 Neutrality Act, he would be blocked from helping China while the cash-and-carry provision allowed Japan to purchase goods in the United States in support of their plans for conquest. Using the discretionary powers granted to him, Roosevelt finessed the situation by refusing to implement the neutrality law on the basis that no official declaration of war existed between Japan and China. To quiet isolationists concerns, Roosevelt prohibited U.S. merchant ships from transporting any armaments to China or Japan. *Time* magazine accurately summarized the predicament the president found himself in by noting that "the scales of public opinion . . . maintained a queasy balance between moral indignation at ruthless international aggression in Spain and China and a feeling that the U.S. must not soil the spirit of peace by taking even a moral stand."[24]

Roosevelt sought to embark on his "longtime education" and start tipping that balance in the direction of internationalism in his Quarantine Speech, delivered in Chicago on October 5, 1937. The importance of the location of the speech cannot be overemphasized because the Windy City, thanks to the virulently anti–New Deal *Chicago Tribune*, was seen as the center of isolationist opinion in the country. There to dedicate the opening of a new bridge, the president surprised his audience by speaking about foreign policy.

Because the Quarantine Speech was Roosevelt's most significant statement of his internationalist understanding of world events and because it marked the beginning of a four-year effort to sway public opinion and confront aggression, it is necessary to quote at length from this speech. Roosevelt began by insisting that the United States must, for its "own future, give thought to the rest of the world" because the developments in Europe and Asia threatened both the security of the nation and its values. The hopes of the Great War, the war to end all wars and make the world safe for democracy, the president stated, had given way to the "present reign of terror and international lawlessness" that started with the "unjustified interference in the internal affairs of other nations" and the "invasion of alien territory in violation of treaties, and has now reached a stage where the very foundations of civilization are seriously threatened. The landmarks and traditions which have marked the progress of civilization towards a condition of law, order and justice are being wiped away."[25]

Turning to Japan's invasion of China, but also capturing the brutality of the war in Spain, Roosevelt noted that without any justification "civilians, including women and children, are being ruthlessly murdered with bombs from the air. . . . Innocent peoples and nations are being cruelly sacrificed to a greed for power and supremacy which is devoid of all sense of justice and humane consideration." If this aggression was not stopped, and the aggressors succeeded, it was folly to think that America could remain immune to the consequences. "Let no one imagine," Roosevelt declared, "that America will escape, that it may expect mercy, that this Western Hemisphere will not be attacked and that it will continue tranquilly and peacefully to carry on the ethics and the arts of civilization."[26]

To avoid war, the "peace-loving nations must make a concerted effort in opposition to those violations of treaties and those ignorings of humane instincts which today are creating a state of international anarchy and instability from which there is no escape through mere isolation or neutrality." Security and morality were intertwined, Roosevelt insisted, and the United States had to work with other nations "for the triumph of law and moral principles in order that peace, justice and confidence may prevail in the world. There must be a return to a belief in the pledged word in the value of a signed treaty. There must be recognition of the fact that national morality is as vital as private morality."[27]

Directly challenging the fundamental assumption of the policy of neutrality to protect the nation from war, the president stated,

> There is a solidarity and interdependence about the modern world, both technically and morally, which makes it impossible for any nation completely to isolate itself from economic and political upheavals in the rest of the world, especially when such upheavals appear to be spreading and not declining. There can be no stability or peace either within nations or between nations except under laws and moral standards adhered to by all. International anarchy destroys every foundation for peace. It jeopardizes either the immediate or the future security of every nation, large or small. It is, therefore, a matter of vital interest and concern to the people of the United States that the sanctity of international treaties and the maintenance of international morality be restored.

Roosevelt contrasted the circumstances that allowed the United States to spend money on bridges, development, and useful works to the growing militarization of some nations that threatened the rest of the world. This was the threat that had to be stopped.[28]

In conclusion, the president argued that war was a contagion that "can engulf states and peoples remote from the original scene of hostilities" and that the "epidemic of world lawlessness is spreading." Nations needed, therefore, to band together and "quarantine" the aggressors to protect the world from the disease's spread. Roosevelt reiterated that he was determined to pursue a policy of peace and keep the nation out of war but that "we cannot insure ourselves against the disastrous effects of war and the dangers of involvement. We are adopting such measures as will minimize our risk of involvement but we cannot have complete protection in a world of disorder in which confidence and security have broken down." The speech ended with the president stating, "America hates war. America hopes for peace. Therefore, America actively engages in the search for peace."[29]

The response to the speech was surprisingly favorable, led by support from the *New York Times*, *Washington Post*, and numerous other papers across the nation which saw the idea of a "quarantine" as a means to stop aggression without war. At a news conference the next day, when asked if he had sanctions in mind, Roosevelt replied, "'sanctions' is a terrible word to use. They are out of the window." The key, he said, was in the last line about the search for peace. "I can't tell you what the methods will be. We are looking for some way to peace."[30] Yet, isolationists and advocates of neutrality offered plenty of criticism, and the president correctly understood that the support for his speech did not mean public support for sanctions against Japan or other steps that might lead to hostilities, as he made clear in an exchange of letters with former Secretary of State Henry L. Stimson.

In November, Stimson, a leading internationalist, wrote Roosevelt with his support for his speech and asked the president to back up his words with action that would enable the United States to lead the world in measures short of war by extending the Stimson Doctrine to include an economic boycott. Japan, he believed, was run by its military and its goals were "inherently hostile" to the United States and its interests. China, he argued, was "fighting our battle for freedom and peace" and to aid it the United States should impose sanctions on Japan to deny it the capacity to wage war.[31]

Roosevelt asked Hull for suggestions on what to say in reply. The president noted that they both "wholly" agreed with Stimson, "but we still have not got an answer." In his response, he told Stimson that his letter stated "considerations which are ever present in my thoughts" but failed to provide him with an acceptable course of action. The Europeans were looking for leadership from the United States, but he was not sure that the "people of this country nor Congress would support any measures of pressure."[32] Roosevelt's letter set out the dilemma he continued to face for the next three years, a desire to take action but an inability to do so because of domestic politics.

On December 12, the U.S. gunboat *Panay*, on patrol in the Yangtze River, was repeatedly bombed and strafed by Japanese planes despite the prominent display of two large American flags, leaving two dead and more than thirty wounded. The American naval presence on the Yangtze dated back to a nineteenth-century treaty with China and was meant to protect American nationals in China. Roosevelt immediately instructed Hull to express to Japan that the nation was shocked and concerned over the indiscriminate bombing of the *Panay*, that the United States was assembling all the facts to present to Tokyo, and that Washington expected a full apology and compensation for the attack and assurances against any future incidents.[33] The president also indicated his willingness to impose sanctions on Japan and consulted with the British on the possibility of a blockade and what further actions might be taken.

Rather than becoming another *Maine* or *Lusitania*, the *Panay* was a quickly forgotten episode. Few demanded more action than the president's call for an apology, and many wondered why the *Panay* was in an area of fighting and called for the withdrawal of American ships from China. This climate of opinion deterred Roosevelt from going forward with any punitive measures and coaxed him to accept the Japanese apology, compensation, and assurances that Americans would be safe in China. So strong was the desire for peace that the incident propelled Representative Louis Ludlow's quixotic quest to transfer the power to declare war from Congress to a national referendum. He introduced a constitutional amendment onto the floor of the House of Representatives for a vote. Polls showed almost 75 percent of the public approved the amendment. Wary of creating a political controversy over a foreign policy issue, Roosevelt, when asked if he thought the amendment was consistent with democratic government, responded, "I suppose the easiest way to answer that is just to say No, and stop there— stop right there."[34] The administration worked hard to block the Ludlow amendment, and it was narrowly defeated in Congress. But the profound fear of war remained a roadblock for the president in trying to craft a policy to curb aggression short of military conflict.

Even without the restraints placed on policymaking by public opinion and Congress, as Roosevelt indicated to Stimson, it was not clear what direction to take. The administration was divided between those who sought to adjust to Japan's actions and find ways of accommodating it in East Asia and those who sought to oppose Japan, impose sanctions, and take a tough line toward Tokyo. These positions were best represented by the two long-time stalwarts of U.S. policy toward Japan, Stanley K. Hornbeck, then the State Department's senior adviser on political relations, and U.S. ambassador to Japan Joseph Grew.

For Hornbeck, the key issue was "that Japan not gain control of China." If that were to happen, the United States and the West would be driven out of East Asia. He, therefore, urged the use of economic sanctions against Japan as the only viable method short of war of stopping Japanese expansion, protecting China, and upholding American interests and the Open Door policy. Japan, Hornbeck believed, had "embarked upon a program of predatory imperialism" that was in direct conflict with the values and legitimate interests of the United States, and unless that march was halted soon, "the time will come when Japan and the United States will be face to face and definitely opposed to each other." If Tokyo's policy of expansion continued, it would mean war. The only way to prevent conflict was to adopt a policy aimed at stopping Japan and averting war. For Hornbeck, the course of necessary action was clear: "The march will be halted only by the power of resistance of material obstacles and material pressures." The problem, of course, was that if the United States took this course of action, it would have to be prepared "to use, if it prove necessary, armed force."[35]

Hornbeck criticized policy up to this point as just the "use of words (appeal to principles, to rules of law, to provisions of treaties, etc.)" that had done little to halt Japan's march into China and designs to dominate the region at the expense of the United States. A continuation of this approach guaranteed a diplomatic defeat and eventual war against an even stronger Japan. Hornbeck, therefore, rejected any notion of appeasement toward Tokyo. "The more we talk and the longer we refrain from resort to some substantial measures of positive (material) pressure toward preventing the Japanese from taking or destroying our rights, titles and interests in the Far East, the more likely will it be that resort by us to such measures at some future time—if and when—will be replied to by the Japanese with resort to armed force against us, which would, in turn, compel us to respond with armed force."[36]

Thus, it was essential, Hornbeck wrote, that the United States provide assistance to China while "withholding those things which are of assistance to the Japanese" in order to strengthen Chinese resistance, prolong the fighting, and weaken Japan. The first step would be to abrogate the 1911 U.S.-Japan commercial treaty; this step would be followed by a repeal of the Neutrality Act, retaliatory tariff measures, an embargo on trade, and U.S. Navy deployment to demonstrate Washington's resolve to protect its interests.[37]

Grew disagreed with these recommendations and warned Washington against imposing economic sanctions. Similar to Hornbeck, Grew was searching for a policy that would protect American interests and prevent war. Grew, however, started from the premise that Japan was in China to stay and that the Open Door could no longer be the basis of American policy. No American action, including a complete embargo on all trade, "would cause the Japanese to relinquish their program in China." They were "inured to hardships" and determined to establish the Greater East Asian Co-Prosperity Sphere. "The so-called 'new order in East Asia' has come to stay," Grew concluded, and there was no chance to create domestic discontent in Japan with the military leaders or deter them from their goals.[38]

Facing these realities, as Grew understood them, the United States had two choices. The first was to try and force Japan to recognize American rights in China through the cancellation of the commercial treaty, an embargo on trade, and aid to China. This, Grew believed, would not work, and in the process, the United States would lose all of its interests in the region and find itself on the path to war.

The second course of action, and the one Grew recommended, was to work with Japan to protect American interests in the new order as much as possible and patiently work with Tokyo to find common ground. This was the only way to protect American commercial and cultural interests in the region and bring future improvement. The worst abuses, Grew believed, such as bombings of properties and "violations of our commercial rights can be stemmed, but unless we are prepared to fight for it, the Open Door, as we conceive it, is not going to be kept open." The choice, therefore, was "losing everything or . . . saving something from the wreckage, while opening the way to a potential building up of our relations with

Japan." Grew proposed offering Japan "a *modus vivendi*" that would provide time for negotiation of a new commercial agreement to create "a material improvement of the situation." Tokyo, he believed, still wanted good relations with Washington, and the United States had a great deal still to lose if a permanent break occurred between the two nations.[39]

Characteristically, Roosevelt choose a middle path: he sought to put some pressure on Japan through increased military spending, aid to China, and an abrogation of the 1911 Commercial Treaty but refused to follow Hornbeck's advice for tariff restrictions, an embargo, and confrontation with Tokyo. In a speech to Congress on January 28, 1938, the president called for a strengthening of the nation's defense as he clearly set out his understanding of the crisis the nation faced, the futility of neutrality, and the need for greater action within the framework of an internationalist policy. Roosevelt began by reminding his audience of the efforts the United States had made over the past two decades to limit and reduce armaments and promote stability. These efforts, however, had failed. New weapons of war were being produced at an unprecedented rate, and wars raged in Europe and Asia that threatened to engulf even more nations. In light of these circumstances, Roosevelt declared that the funding and equipment for the military was "inadequate for purposes of national security."[40]

Directly challenging the fundamental assumptions of the proponents of neutrality, FDR argued that "adequate defense means that for the protection not only of our coasts but also of our communities far removed from the coast, we must keep any potential enemy many hundred miles away from our continental limits. We cannot assume that our defense would be limited to one ocean and one coast and that the other ocean and the other coast would with certainty be safe." The president, therefore, had a duty to promote peace but also to "protect our Nation." In effect, Roosevelt was arguing that Europe and Asia were the front lines of American defense as he called for increased spending for battleships, cruisers, and other ships for the navy, and money for antiaircraft material and a larger army reserve.[41]

Gerald P. Nye led the congressional opposition to Roosevelt's proposal. He argued that the proper defense of the nation was based on the distance the two oceans provided from hostile nations and protecting the Western Hemisphere. Increased spending would move the United States closer to war, Nye argued, as it was designed to allow the nation to fight thousands of miles away from home and would entangle it in foreign wars.

Yet, Japan's attack on China and Germany's increasing belligerence had raised concerns about national defense and the need for military preparedness and had eroded the support for isolation. Congress passed a munitions bill in May that provided a 20 percent increase in naval spending and funds to fortify bases in the Pacific Ocean. The bill was not enough to deter Japan, but its passage indicated that Roosevelt was starting to gain the upper hand in the battles over how to define national security and for public support of his policies.

As it became clear in 1938 that Chaing Kai-shek's nationalist government was running out of money, the Roosevelt administration arranged the so-called Tung Oil loan worth $100 million. The loan was not for the actual purchase of tung oil but rather was a war loan in disguise. The United States sent the full $100 million for tung or wood oil, which China could spend right away on the war effort, but would not receive the oil until some future time when China was able to send it. As Cordell Hull noted, the money was a symbolic and political action rather than a step that would change the military equation, but the president supported it because it indicated that he sought to help victims of aggression, was part of his larger efforts to put pressure on Japan, and sent the right message to the American people as Roosevelt sought to build public support for China.

More important, the president served notice to Tokyo that Washington would not renew the 1911 Commercial Treaty between Japan and the United States. The Roosevelt administration notified Japan in July 1939 that it was terminating the agreement, which officially expired in January 1940. Grew and others argued that sanctions would not deter Japan, but the Asian nation did rely heavily on American oil and scrap metal for its military machine and so was vulnerable to decisions made in Washington as the United States supplied 50 percent of its petroleum, iron, and copper, all essential for military operations. The ending of the treaty would make it legally possible for the administration to impose sanctions or an embargo on Japan without congressional approval.

The Beginning of the End of Neutrality

The outbreak of war in Europe in September 1939 led to a significant revision of the Neutrality Act and the repeal of the arms embargo as the president sought greater freedom of action in his ability to respond to the rapidly expanding crisis. In his State of the Union speech in January 1939, Roosevelt had focused on the growing international crisis, the threat it presented to the United States, and the need to revise America's neutrality laws to allow aid to nations facing aggression abroad. In his most direct attack on the logic of neutrality, the president declared, "We have learned that when we deliberately try to legislate neutrality, our neutrality laws may operate unevenly and unfairly—may actually give aid to an aggressor and deny it to the victim." The only way to prevent attack was "an ever ready defense," preparedness, and cooperation with like-minded countries.[42]

What was at stake, Roosevelt declared, was both the physical security of the nation and its values. While the Western Hemisphere was united by the Good Neighbor policy, mutual respect, and a desire for peace, the world, the president stated, "has grown small and weapons of attack so swift that no nation can be safe in its will to peace as long as any other single powerful nation refuses to settle its grievances at the council table" regardless of the nation's location. But even if the United States was not under direct attack, institutions and values that were essential to the nation and to the promotion of peace, specifically freedom of religion, democracy, and respect for laws, were being undermined overseas. The dictatorships of Germany, Japan, and Italy sought to destroy these and in doing so were creating a world that was hostile to the United States and that would eventually cause it harm. This necessitated armed forces strong enough to defend the nation and "ensure sustained resistance and ultimate victory," and a nation united to defend itself and its beliefs.[43]

Any chance for peace short of war, Roosevelt insisted, would come through military preparedness, cooperation with Great Britain, and a clear statement to the dictators that U.S. resources would not lie idle if fighting began. The United States could not avoid the negative consequences of war or remain neutral once it came. The false hope that the proponents of neutrality and isolation held out, that the United States could remain safe within its own hemisphere or continental boundaries, was based on an erroneous understanding of the fascist governments. The dictatorships were the antithesis of Western civilization's values and could not be reached through reason and diplomacy. They not only scorned the values of freedom, democracy, and rule by law but sought to destroy their neighbors who held such views. In such circumstances, Roosevelt insisted, treating all nations the same was not only impossible but also dangerous and the height of folly. Any further efforts at neutrality would be disastrous for all nations.

With German and Japanese aggression mounting, public opinion in the United States began to shift in 1939. In March, Germany, breaking the agreement made at Munich, annexed the rest of Czechoslovakia. Great Britain finally abandoned appeasement and along with France provided assurances to Poland that it would come to its aid if attacked by Germany. Still, the Western nations were unwilling to include the Soviet Union in a collective security arrangement and spurned the final efforts by Moscow to reach an agreement for joint defense. With the German annexation of Czechoslovakia, for the first time a majority of the American people favored providing Great Britain and France with weapons, planes, and other war supplies, and the Roosevelt administration asked Congress to amend the Neutrality Act to end the arms embargo provision.

The administration fought with isolationists and proponents of neutrality throughout the summer of 1939 to get Congress to enact a new law. When the Senate Foreign Relations Committee voted in July to defer any action until January, Roosevelt sent a direct message written by Hull calling for immediate action to be read in Congress. The key point of the message was that the only way for the United States to stay out of war now was to allow it to send arms to the democracies threatened by Germany and Japan. A continuation of the arms embargo "plays into the hands of those nations which have taken the lead in building up their fighting power. It works directly against the interests of the peace-loving nations."[44] Four days later, Roosevelt met with Senate leaders to encourage them to reconsider the bill. Holding to their position that arms sales would drag the nation into war and that neutrality was the best means to preserve peace, the senators remained opposed to any repeal of the arms embargo. Senator William Borah went so far as to claim that there would be no war in Europe in the near future and argued that any changes would foster war rather than prevent it.

The headlong rush to war in Europe did not hinge on the Senate's decisions regarding neutrality. In August, Germany and the Soviet Union shocked the world with the announcement of the Nazi-Soviet nonaggression pact, which assured Germany it would not have to fight a two-front war when it attacked Poland. The German invasion came on September 1, 1939. Speaking to the nation on September 3, the day Great Britain and France declared war on Germany, Roosevelt noted that the United States would be officially neutral, meaning the nation could not sell armaments and key war supplies to the Allies, but that he could not ask people to be neutral in their thoughts as no one could ignore who the aggressor was or their own conscience.

The war in Europe, the president stated, would affect every American and the nation's well-being, and the laws of the nation needed to reflect that reality. With this in mind, FDR called for a special session of Congress to amend the neutrality laws and repeal the arms embargo. Such an action, he opined, represented perhaps the last hope to prevent the United States from being dragged into the new conflagration. Although isolationists mounted an all-out campaign to defeat any revisions, they were no longer strong enough to prevent the change. Roosevelt's arguments that it was both the moral and materially correct course of action to assist Great Britain and France, who were fighting America's battle, had won. In November, Roosevelt signed the new law that allowed the president to provide aid to the opponents of fascism and repealed the arms embargo.

With war in Europe and Asia, Roosevelt now faced a new set of problems. He knew that the triumph over the restrictive neutrality laws did not mean that the nation was ready to join the war or that it should. To be sure, there had been movement in the public willingness to provide aid to the victims of German aggression, but the vast majority of the American people still opposed the United States going to war. Yet, American policy was now solidly based on preparedness and cooperation with the Allies. The new problems were how to aid the Western democracies and how deeply to get involved in the war. On these matters, Roosevelt was very aware of the public's desire to stay out of war, and he knew he still had to convince them of the last part of his internationalist vision, taking on the role of world leader and direct participation in the global struggle against fascism.

CHAPTER 4

THE TRIUMPH OF
INTERNATIONALISM

THE OUTBREAK OF WAR IN EUROPE BROUGHT THE FINAL REVISIONS of the Neutrality Act that President Roosevelt sought, but it did not solve the larger problems that confronted the nation abroad. The questions facing the president were, how could the United States increase aid to Great Britain and France without getting too far ahead of public support, and how could he increase American preparedness without causing alarm that he planned to take the nation to war? Despite having picked sides in terms of their willingness to aid the Western democracies, the American public remained overwhelmingly opposed to U.S. participation in the war and feared being dragged into the fighting through direct support. The war in Europe was the top priority of the administration as the German threat was greatest to American interests, but the potential of a Japanese attack on the Western colonies in Southeast Asia provided a direct link between the wars in Europe and East Asia and made the conflict, as President Roosevelt saw it, a world war that demanded a global strategy for national defense. Given this, in 1940 the issue was how much pressure to place on Japan after the termination of the commercial treaty without provoking Tokyo to expand the war's scope. Roosevelt did not want to imperil the Europeans' access to the wealth and resources of their colonies, and thus their ability to resist Germany, but he also could not allow Japan to grow stronger and increase its threat to the United States.

Events in Europe in 1940 and the formation of the Axis alliance resolved parts of these problems, and by the summer of 1940, Roosevelt began taking a series of steps that provided essential aid to Great Britain, prepared the United States for war, and set it on a collision course with Japan. From June 1940 to March 1941, the president put into place his war cabinet, obtained direct aid for Great Britain through lend-lease, and imposed a partial embargo on Japan. This was the crucial period during which Roosevelt's efforts to persuade the American public to follow his internationalist policy succeeded as the nation abandoned neutrality and isolationism for collective security and world leadership as the only means to defend the nation and its interests. While war was still six months off, the basis for American participation had been established and accepted by the American people.

Throughout the summer and fall of 1941, Roosevelt moved the country toward war as events confirmed for the American public the correctness of Roosevelt's policy. The German invasion of the Soviet Union in June and Japan's taking of all of Indochina in July widened the war further and made clear the global threat posed by the Axis. In response to the Axis's maneuvers, Roosevelt extended American aid to the Soviet Union, thus creating the Grand Alliance against Germany, and solidified the alliance with Great Britain through the Atlantic Charter. In East Asia, the president concluded that American interests, in both Europe and the Pacific, could be protected only through war with Japan. He, therefore, extended the embargo to include oil and maneuvered with Japan to make sure that its attacks were to the south and that it was clear who the aggressor was in the coming of American participation in World War II.

Mobilization

After Germany's quick defeat and dismemberment of Poland, fighting stopped on the ground in Europe for the winter of 1939–1940. The Allies used this time of the so-called phony war to mobilize, plan, and prepare their defenses in the West. By 1940, with no battles in more than three months, many hoped that a negotiated end might be found that would spare the continent further warfare. President Roosevelt, while skeptical of any real chances for peace with Hitler and believing that the odds of a negotiated peace were next to nonexistent, nonetheless was willing to explore any avenue that might prevent the massive destruction of a European war. More significant, the president hoped to aid the Allies and to take advantage of Italy's nonbelligerent status to split the Axis and thereby contain the fighting to northern Europe. Roosevelt believed the Allies would win but only after a long and bitter contest that would bring economic and social collapse to Europe. Thus, in February 1940, he sent Sumner Welles to Europe to evaluate the prospects for peace and to try and persuade Benito Mussolini to keep Italy at least neutral if not to again get it to switch sides, as Rome had in 1915.

Welles made Italy the first and last stop on his European mission. He told the Italian dictator that Roosevelt was pleased that he had maintained the peace in the Mediterranean and Balkan areas, was sympathetic to Italy's needs, and hoped to meet with Il Duce some day. Although Welles's mission officially called for him to evaluate only the prospects of a just and durable negotiated peace, he was determined to find a way to break Rome away from Berlin by persuading Mussolini that Italy's interests would be better served if it cooperated with the United States and its support of the Allies. If Rome cooperated, Washington would be sure to help Italy obtain the concessions it sought in any peace agreement. While no agreement was reached, and Welles saw no chance for a negotiated peace, when he returned home in March he was optimistic that Italy's influence would be to limit the war's spread.

When Hitler invaded Denmark and Norway on April 9, 1940, the matter of keeping Italy out of the war became urgent. In April and May, Roosevelt sent Mussolini four messages asking him to remain neutral. In each, the president praised Italy's restraint up to this point. Hoping to force Mussolini to look beyond Germany's early victories, the president made it clear that he believed Germany would ultimately lose the war and that any further spread of the war would harm significant American interests and lead to American intervention. "No man," Roosevelt wrote, "can today predict with assurances, should further extension take place . . . what nations, however determined they may be today to remain at peace, might yet eventually find it imperative in their own defense to enter the war."[1] Italy, to be spared the ordeal of war and for its own interests, should remain neutral and/or side with the Allies or expect defeat. The threat could not have been made clearer.

Germany's lightning attack in May 1940 into the Low Countries and France brought an end to the so-called phony war, made it clear that Italy was going to join Germany in the war, and led President Roosevelt to take a series of steps in response to the German victories. In just six weeks, Belgium, Holland, Luxembourg, and France fell, leaving Great Britain to fight the Axis alone. With Italy's declaration of war on June 10 and attack on France that day, the rest of Europe was plunged into the fighting. From the Russian border in the east to the Atlantic coast, Nazi Germany and its allies controlled Europe, and only the British navy and air force stood between the United States and the Nazi juggernaut.

Speaking at the University of Virginia on the day Italy entered the war, Roosevelt declared, "On this tenth day of June, 1940, the hand that held the dagger has struck it into the back of its neighbor." In response to the Axis attacks, the president made his boldest ever statement on the war. The United States, he declared, would follow two simultaneous courses of action: "We will extend to the opponents of force the material resources of the nation; and, at the same time, we will harness and speed up the use of those resources in order that we ourselves in the Americas may have equipment and training equal to the task of any emergency and every defense."[2] Roosevelt was now prepared to act on the position he had been trying to convince the American people was necessary, a policy of collective security, aid to Great Britain, and taking up the role of world leader.

To back up his words, Roosevelt asked Congress for dramatic increases in defense funding totaling over twelve billion dollars by the end of 1940. The shock of France's quick fall had a significant impact on the American public's views of the danger Nazi Germany posed and opened the door for Roosevelt to take bolder moves to aid Great Britain. As Congress passed the appropriations bills to finance a larger military and more weapons, Roosevelt established a war cabinet to help him create bipartisan support for his policies. On June 19, the president asked former Secretary of War and Secretary of State Henry L. Stimson to be secretary of war and Frank Knox to be secretary of the navy. Both men were leading Republicans who supported the president's policies. Stimson was the more notable of the two and was known as a leading internationalist and advocate of mobilization and aid to Great Britain. Indeed, Stimson was well ahead of the president in terms of publicly calling for greater American involvement in the war against Hitler. It was imperative, he believed, that the United States repeal the remaining neutrality laws and openly supply England with anything it needed, including access to American ports, planes, and munitions. Moreover, Stimson called for the beginning of a draft to further American preparedness, greater production of munitions and planes, and U.S. naval convoys to protect supplies crossing the Atlantic.

The administration faced an array of challenges in the summer of 1940 as the president continued his effort to aid Britain and prepare the nation for war. The rearmament program was just starting and the United

States was not yet able to provide the number of supplies a desperate Great Britain needed to ensure its defense. Simultaneously, Japan moved to take advantage of Germany's victories in Europe by moving into the French colony of Indochina to strengthen its ability to fight in southern China, gain more raw materials, and improve its position in Southeast Asia. This maneuver created a threat to all Western colonies in the region. Finally, there remained the domestic political battles, upcoming election in which FDR sought an unprecedented third term, and the task of persuading the nation of its obligation for world leadership and a new definition of national security in the face of the global crisis.

To meet these problems, Roosevelt acted to increase the nation's defense. Throughout the summer, the administration worked to gain passage of the Selective Service Bill. There had never been a peacetime draft in American history, and the administration had to overcome this legacy along with opponents' arguments that the bill would increase the risk of war. Speaking for the administration, Secretary of War Stimson argued that voluntary enlistment left the army well below its authorized strength and that the draft was the only fair and democratic means to raise a modern army and meet the nation's security needs. The administration's efforts succeeded, and President Roosevelt signed the Selective Service Act on September 16, 1940. With the president looking on, Stimson drew the first numbers in the draft lottery on October 29. To organize and lead the new expanded army called for by this legislation, the military established officer candidate schools to train its larger officer corps.

Simultaneously, the administration was searching for means to get desperately needed military equipment to Great Britain. While the United States had begun massive new production programs of planes, tanks, and other weapons, the new equipment would not begin to appear in large volumes until the end of the year. The United States did possess, however, two hundred old destroyers from World War I, which were in storage and for which the navy had little need. In August, Knox suggested to Roosevelt that he trade fifty of these for eight British bases in Greenland, the West Indies, and the Atlantic coast of Canada. Announced on September 3, the president presented the destroyers-for-bases deal as the "most important action in the reinforcement of our national defense that has been taken since the Louisiana Purchase. Then as now, considerations of safety from overseas attack were fundamental."[3]

The deal marked a turning point in the administration's efforts to

Roosevelt discusses the Greer incident during a fireside chat on September 11, 1941.
Franklin D. Roosevelt Library

support England and set out the U.S. stake in Nazi Germany's defeat. The American public, its sympathy for Great Britain bolstered by the British people's heroic resistance to the German bombings of its cities, broadly supported this first direct military aid to Great Britain, and the swapping of destroyers for British bases served as a precursor for the logic and appeal of the president's lend-lease policy. With the Axis on the offensive around the globe and reports of the suffering inflicted at their hand a daily event, Americans in larger and larger numbers came to see their actions as a threat and concluded that the United States was not as safe as they once thought. The protests of isolationists and those who demanded neutrality had fallen mute. Moreover, Roosevelt was able to get the public to see the actions of German fascism and Japanese militarism as part of the same crisis, merging them together in the public mind as dangerous, evil, and cruel forms of government that were the antithesis of American values and the progress of civilization. Japan's official announcement of its intention to create an East Asian economic block, the Greater East Asian Co-Prosperity Sphere, and to move its forces into the French colony of Indochina in June 1940, served to cement the view that the totalitarian and aggressive natures of Tokyo and Berlin were the same. A story in *Time* magazine that summer, headlined "Japan: Imitation of Naziism?" further bolstered this view.[4]

Japan was clearly taking advantage of the German victories in Europe to bring its dream of dominating East Asia to fruition, and its attack on Southeast Asia demanded an American response. Stanley Hornbeck set out the issue facing the United States on July 19, when he called for action from the administration in response to Japan's move to the south. "If Japan gets possession of huge new supplies . . . her embarkation upon carrying out of new acts of aggression will be greatly facilitated. If action is taken on our part which results in failure on Japan's part to receive these new supplies," Hornbeck continued, "such action and the resultant failure might retard or prevent such new adventuring and would certainly make it . . . more difficult."[5] It was clear to all senior administration officials that continued patience and restraint would encourage more expansion and that the

Roosevelt signs the Selective Service Act on September 16, 1940. Looking on are (left to right) Secretary of War Henry L. Stimson, Representative Andrew Jackson May, Gen. George Marshall, and Senator Morris Shepard. Franklin D. Roosevelt Library

time had come to move beyond aid to China and to directly oppose Japan. Following Hornbeck's recommendation, in September Roosevelt approved an embargo on trading iron, scrap metal, and other materials that could be used in war with Japan. Omitted from the list of goods was oil. Japan imported nearly 50 percent of its supply from the United States and its war machine could not function without it. The president, however, feared that cutting off oil at that time would drive Japan to attack the Dutch East Indies (Indonesia) to secure its supply, a move the president wanted to delay or prevent if possible to keep the wealth of this area available to Great Britain.

Roosevelt's actions found widespread support among the American people that fall and were bolstered by groups such as the Committee to Defend America by Aiding the Allies, a nonpartisan group founded by the Kansas editor William Allen White to mobilize support for Roosevelt's foreign policy. Through hundreds of chapters in all states, the committee took up the main themes of the president's internationalist arguments, mainly the need to aid Great Britain, increase America's strength, control the Atlantic Ocean, prevent subversive actions by America's enemies in the Western Hemisphere, and protect democracy and American values in the world. The German air attacks on British cities that fall also served to rally American support for Roosevelt's efforts to aid Great Britain and to highlight the threat the president claimed faced the nation. The German blitz confirmed the picture of an aggressive, brutal state determined to destroy democratic institutions and values.

Roosevelt's Republican challenger, Wendell Willkie, supported most of Roosevelt's defense measures and initiatives taken that summer and fall. This left it to the newly created America First Committee (AFC) to provide the opposition to Roosevelt's policies. Basing its arguments on the view that the oceans provided the protection America needed, the America First Committee supported preparedness but not aid to Great Britain. Peace and American freedoms, the AFC argued, could be preserved only by keeping out of any involvement in the war in Europe. Aid would just drag the nation into another European war and repeat the mistakes made during World War I. Rather than wasting resources by sending them abroad, the United States should build itself up so that no nation would dare try to attack it. There was little new in this position, but the arguments that had been so persuasive throughout most of the 1930s were now, in the face of Axis aggression, no longer convincing to most Americans.

Toward the end of the campaign, Willkie did try to distance himself from Roosevelt by claiming that he supported measures necessary for defense but that the president, if reelected, intended to take the nation into the war. The Republican candidate promised that he would not send American boys to fight foreign wars. Roosevelt responded on October 30 in Boston by declaring, "I have said this before, but I shall say it again and again. Your boys are not going to be sent into any foreign wars." So close to the election, the president dropped the qualifying phrase "except in the case of attack," which he usually added, so as to not raise fears that Willkie's charges were correct.[6] Roosevelt had decided to run for a third term only because of the war in Europe, and it was the nation's confidence in his ability to handle that crisis as he had the Great Depression that led them to return him to Pennsylvania Avenue for another term.

Lend-Lease

With the election over and the danger of a British defeat ever present, the administration began to take more active steps to prepare the public for what many now saw as the inevitability of American participation in the war. The president's position, shared by his senior staff, was that Nazi Germany provided the greatest threat and that Europe, not Asia, had to be the primary concern. The appropriations secured throughout 1940 were beginning to show dividends as large amounts of war matériel was being produced by the end of the year. But as supplies became available in December, two new problems confronted the administration. American laws restricted the administration's ability to transfer weapons to another nation, and Great Britain was going broke and unable to pay, as cash-and-carry required, for the materials and munitions it needed to hold off the Germans. In a lengthy letter sent on December 8, British prime minister Winston Churchill outlined the British shortages in weapons, ships, and plans, the devastating losses being suffered at sea from German attacks, and the fast approaching exhaustion of British financial ability to purchase goods from the United States. American officials had been aware of British needs but not the full extent of the coming crisis that would occur if no new action was taken.

Roosevelt broke the logjam with his call for lend-lease. Speaking to reporters on December 17, the president stated the key point of his developing national security policy, that the "best immediate defense of the United States is the success of Great Britain in defending itself." Acutely aware of the problems with loans and credits, the difficulties this issue caused during and after World War I, and the fact that financial aid was a touchstone of the neutrality laws and isolationist opinion, the president presented a novel approach to the issue of how to aid England. "Now, what I am trying to do," the president explained, is "get rid of the silly, foolish old dollar sign." To explain what he meant, Roosevelt used his since famous garden hose analogy, noting that if your neighbor's house is on fire, and they lack a hose to put it out, you would lend your hose to them and worry about any damage or costs later. Similarly, the United States would supply Great Britain with the necessary supplies for winning the war "with the understanding that when the show was over, we would get repaid something in kind, thereby leaving out the dollar mark in the form of a dollar debt and substituting for it a gentleman's obligation to repay in kind."[7]

On December 29, in his first fireside chat since the election, Roosevelt gave substance to what this meant and pledged all-out aid to England through the Lend-Lease Act. In doing so, FDR made the case that American security could be secured only through alliances with others, by providing global leaderships, and through a willingness to fight just wars that would defend and spread American values and institutions. Roosevelt began by stating that his fireside chat was not on the topic of war but national security. He compared the world crisis facing the nation with the domestic crisis it faced eight years earlier and called upon the American people to face this new crisis with the same courage and forthright manner it demonstrated in 1933. Never before, Roosevelt declared, had "our American civilization been in such danger as now." The threat the Axis nations posed was clear as Germany intended to "enslave the whole of Europe, and then to use the resources of Europe to dominate the rest of the world." The world was bipolar, the president declared, divided between the totalitarian powers led by Hitler and his declared contempt for democracy and those who opposed his aggression and threat to civilization. The Axis, Roosevelt stated, "not merely admits but proclaims that there can be no ultimate peace between their philosophy of government and our philosophy of government." With such a government and its use of force there could be no peace until the aggressor nations were defeated in their quest to conquer the world. The only thing currently keeping them away from America was the British in the Atlantic and China and the American fleet in the Pacific.[8]

The president then took up the neutralist argument that the wars in Europe and Asia were not America's concern, that the oceans would insulate the nation, and that the hemisphere was the only proper area of defense. Bluntly, he declared that this was pure folly. He rhetorically asked if anyone believed that the Western Hemisphere would be safe if Germany defeated Great Britain. Modern bombers had made the oceans obsolete as a singular basis of defense, and German agents and other subversive elements were already at work trying to undermine many of the American republics. Moreover, a British defeat would open up the oceans to the Axis and allow them to establish bases in the Western Hemisphere. "If Great Britain goes down," Roosevelt warned, "the Axis Powers will control the continents of Europe, Asia, Africa, Australasia, and the high seas—and they will be in a position to bring enormous military and naval resources against this hemisphere. It is no exaggeration to say that all of us in the Americas would be living at the point of a gun." To understand what that would mean, one needed only to look at the nations in Europe the Nazis had already conquered.[9]

Complacent neutralists would counter, Roosevelt noted, that the Nazis and Japanese would have no desire to attack North and South America. That, the president believed, was wishful thinking belied by all the evidence and proclamations of the Axis governments to destroy all who opposed them. No nation can negotiate with or appease the Nazis. "There can be no appeasement with ruthlessness," Roosevelt proclaimed, adding, "a nation can have peace with the Nazis only at the price of total surrender." Those who still urged negotiations and accommodation, Roosevelt noted, who claimed that Germany would win anyway and that the United States should make the best of it, called that approach a negotiated peace. "Nonsense!" the president declared. This was surrender to dictatorship and the illusion of peace. The only way to possibly still keep the United States out of war was to support Great Britain and others currently fighting the Axis. If "we acquiesce in their defeat, submit tamely to an Axis victory," then the United States will just be waiting "our turn to be the object of attack in another war later on."[10]

In the end, the president argued that the war was not just America against the Axis, but democracy against world tyranny. The United States, he declared, "must be the great arsenal of democracy." Only the productive capacity of the United States to build more ships, guns, planes, and munitions, and the will of the American people to meet the world crisis and the threat to U.S. security would turn the tide and ensure victory over the dictators.[11]

The final piece of the president's effort to build support for his policies and define the meaning of the war for the United States came in his
State of the Union message to Congress on January 6, 1941. Devoted
completely to the international crisis, the need to aid Britain, and the meaning of the war for the United States, Roosevelt's speech started with his now
familiar theme that the moment in time was unprecedented in the history
of the nation as the nation's security was for the first time threatened from
without. "The democratic way of life," Roosevelt declared, "is at this moment being directly assailed in every part of the world," including the United
States, and it was incumbent upon the nation to act with resolve and speed
in meeting this attack. The president, therefore, urged Congress to pass the
lend-lease bill. "Let us say to the democracies: America stands behind you.
America is putting forth her energies, her resources and her organizing
powers to give you the strength to regain and maintain a free world. America
will send you, in ever-increasing numbers, ships, planes, tanks and guns,
food and medical supplies."[12]

In calling for sacrifice from the nation, Roosevelt told his audience
the goal was not only victory over the Axis but also the creation of a better
world. He concluded his remarks by looking forward to the postwar world,
a "world founded fundamentally upon four essential human freedoms":
freedom of speech, freedom of worship, freedom from want, and freedom
from fear. This was not a distant dream but a goal to attain "in our own time
and generation." It was the antithesis of the world the Axis sought to create,
but it was the world that could be created through American productive
capacity, values and institutions, and willingness to take on the role of world
leadership. Acting upon the goal of protecting and spreading freedom,
Roosevelt concluded, "There can be no end save victory."[13] The president
had staked out a global vision of national security, American world leadership, and a postwar order based on American values across the world. The
"Great Debate" over lend-lease and the definition of American national
security policy had begun.

The lend-lease bill, numbered House Resolution 1776 and called by
its supporters "a bill further to promote the defense of the United States,"
was introduced on January 10, 1941. For the next two months it was at the
center of an intense national debate about the specific request but, more
important, about U.S. foreign policy and the best means to provide for the
nation's national security. By the time the legislation was introduced,
Roosevelt's arguments on behalf of lend-lease gave it the support of a

majority of the American public and members of Congress. Still, the president wanted a full debate to further build support, to allow certain amendments to allay the fears of those who had reservations, and to show that the administration was listening to its critics. In the process Roosevelt hoped to create a broad consensus among the American people in favor of lend-lease and his understanding of America's role in the war being fought in Europe.

The administration and its allies framed the debate as one about national security, defense, and responsibility to upholding certain values and world order. They repeated the key points the president had made in his recent talks to the nation, emphasizing Axis aggression, the crucial need to sustain Great Britain to contain the German threat, and the infeasibility, given modern air power and subversion, of dependence on a hemispheric defense. Lend-lease was, therefore, vital to the nation's defense and protection of democracy because if Germany defeated England, it would only be a matter of time before Hitler attacked the United States.

A number of groups and individuals fervently opposed the measure, including leading senators such as Bennett Clark, Gerald Nye, Robert Taft, Arthur Vandenburg, and Burton Wheeler, the America First Committee, and aviator Charles Lindbergh. They believed that the bill gave the president too much power, bordering on dictatorial control over the economy; that it would pull the United States into the war, not keep it out; and that it would harm America's ability to defend itself by sending vital goods and equipment overseas. Central to all of these arguments was World War I as an example of why the United States should avoid all European wars. Opponents noted that those debts had yet to be repaid, that there was the question of how the goods would get to England without naval escorts given the presence of German submarines, and that no vital American interests had been secured or protected in World War I and there was no reason to think the outcome of the current war would be any different. Moreover, they claimed that Great Britain still had plenty of assets that it could use to buy supplies and that it was just trying to get the American taxpayer to subsidize the fighting and American boys to do the fighting. Given this, the America First Committee and its allies argued that lend-lease was not about aiding England or defense but about getting the United States directly involved in the war.

Senator Nye, the president's longtime nemesis, led the opposition once again. He believed that Roosevelt was lying to the American people about his intentions and that the bill was aimed at taking the nation to war. If the president was honest, he declared, he would call it "a bill to put the United States fully into the bloody business of licking Adolf Hitler."[14] Taft agreed, noting that the bill would allow Roosevelt to become the "great protagonist of the forces opposing Hitler" as it was a virtual declaration of war. "There is here no question of appeasement," Taft continued. "Appeasement means the yielding to demands with the hope that such yielding will prevent further aggression." Yet, "Germany has made no demands on the United States; has made no attack on the United States."[15]

Clark claimed that the lend-lease bill, rather than promoting U.S. defense, would "authorize the denuding of American defenses; . . . authorize the suspension of any American law inconsistent with the dictatorial powers conferred in the proposed act; . . . authorize the . . . supplying of any country . . . at the expense of the American taxpayers; . . . authorize the underwriting of the cost of maintaining the British Empire . . . [and] bring the war to our very doors; to abandon the Monroe Doctrine by the abandonment of its vital principle of not participating in Europe's wars."[16]

Lindbergh, speaking on behalf of the America First Committee, attacked the logic of Roosevelt's claims that lend-lease would aid the nation's defense. He claimed, on the one hand, that Germany would defeat Great Britain no matter what the United States did. There was, therefore, no use in trying to prevent it. Moreover, all the aid sent would just go to waste. On the other hand, Lindbergh questioned the president's claims that the nation would be in danger from long-range bombers and argued that any air attacks would be futile and that Germany could not conquer the United States that way. He insisted that hemispheric defense remained a viable idea and the best protection for the nation as it would deter any Axis attack.

Secretary of War Stimson took the lead in presenting the administration's case. Testifying five separate times before Congress, Stimson argued that passage of the Lend-Lease Act was vital to America's defense as it would provide order to the current chaotic system of procuring weapons for the Allies, permit the government to exercise centralized control over weapons production, and allow the president the full authority he needed in the time of national emergency. Preparedness, planning, defense, support of Great Britain, and maximized production, not the fear of presidential power or antagonizing Germany, were the main issues, the secretary of war told the legislatures.

Prior to the final vote, opponents were able to secure some important amendments, including a time limit on the bill; periodic reports to Congress by the administration on the amount of spending, type of goods, and shipment records; and a statement that the act did not authorize U.S. naval escorts to protect shipping. None of these, however, changed the act's main components or the direction in which the president was taking the nation. In the end, on March 11 the Lend-Lease Act easily passed in both houses of Congress, 60-31 in the Senate and 260-165 in the House. The law allowed the president to "sell, transfer title to, exchange, lease, lend, or otherwise dispose of" any defense article to any government deemed vital to U.S defense and thus provided Roosevelt with legal authority over all military supplies.

The United States had in effect declared economic war on Germany and made available its wealth and vast resources for the battle. The War Department was well prepared for the bill's passage and the first supplies were shipped out right after Roosevelt signed the legislation. U.S. national security was now directly tied to an internationalist policy of supporting Great Britain, working with allies, and victory over Hitler in Europe.

Secretary of War Stimson draws the first number in the draft lottery, October 29, 1940.
Franklin D. Roosevelt Library

The Battle of the Atlantic

The president's critics were right on one point in the debate: the passage of lend-lease was a turning point because it demanded naval escorts and placed the nation on the road to war. This new policy, however, was in line with the public's understanding of the crisis. Opinion polls showed the full extent of the president's achievement as two-thirds of the public favored the bill. Moreover, 70 percent of the American people thought the president's policies were "about right" or had not gone far enough to help Great Britain. While a year before a large majority had said it was more important to stay out of the war than to aid Great Britain, by the spring of 1941 nearly 60 percent said sending aid to England, even if it meant the United States might be drawn into the war, was essential and should be American policy.[17]

For lend-lease to be effective, it was necessary to save the British lifeline in the North Atlantic. A commitment of the U.S. Navy to protect shipping and the movement of lend-lease supplies was vital to prevent a German victory. Noting the staggering losses in shipping—over four million tons of Allied and neutral shipping in 1940—caused by German submarines, Stimson urged Roosevelt to forcibly stop the Germans by using the navy to escort all supplies to English ports to ensure Great Britain's survival. The president, however, was not yet ready to take such a bold step; he feared Congress would refuse to grant him the power to convoy ships and in the process revitalize the neutralist position, undermine his recent achievements and effort to gradually prepare the nation for war, and at the same time harm British morale. The president had good reasons for his caution: an anti-convoy measure had already been introduced in Congress and he did not know if the naval buildup had reached the point where the navy could carry out a full convoy without weakening the fleet in the Pacific and emboldening the Japanese.

Roosevelt announced in April that the United States would patrol the western half of the Atlantic Ocean, extending in the north as far as Iceland, thus freeing the British navy to concentrate on the waters closer to home. This measure was accepted as it was portrayed as a defensive move to keep watch for hostile actions close to home. As the president noted in a cabinet meeting, the navy patrol was another "step forward" toward meeting the German danger, but Roosevelt was still willing to wait on circumstances to bring about conflict before he asked for bolder steps from Congress.[18]

While the president was unwilling to go any further, he allowed Stimson to state the case for war in a national radio address the next month. The secretary of war bluntly declared that he was not one who believed that the "priceless freedom of our country can be saved without sacrifice." It was necessary to acknowledge that Germany was an enemy that was determined to destroy the freedom of all nations and that U.S. security and future prosperity depended upon its defeat. "Unless we on our side are ready to sacrifice," Stimson warned, "and, if need be, die for the conviction that the freedom of America must be saved, it will not be saved. Only by a readiness for the same sacrifice can that freedom be preserved."[19] Stimson was the most outspoken interventionist in the administration and his speech marked the administration's boldest statement of this position and the first public statement of the case for the United States entering the war by a senior official.

No matter what actions the United States took, the news from Europe continued to worsen. In April and May, Germany gained almost complete control over the Balkans while the destruction of shipping continued to rise, with over 680,000 tons lost in April alone. The situation became so desperate that in May, British prime minister Churchill telegraphed Roosevelt asking for the first time that the United States declare war on Germany and become a belligerent. Stimson and other senior officials urged the president to take the lead, make the case for war, and rally the nation to the necessity of defeating Germany. While Stimson was sure the nation would support Roosevelt if he sought a declaration of war, the president was not and remained committed to taking gradual steps.

On May 27, Roosevelt declared an unlimited national emergency, placing all military forces on readiness to defend the nation and the Western Hemisphere. That evening, he explained his action to the nation and set out an expanded vision of America's proper defense sphere and national security requirements. He recalled for the American people the constant path of aggression that Nazi Germany had followed with the aim of world conquest and said that Germany would not stop until it was defeated. He also reviewed the measures he had taken up to then to defend the nation, from concluding agreements with the other American republics for hemispheric defense to the rearmament program, naval buildup, draft, and lend-lease policies of the past year. At stake, Roosevelt reminded his listeners, was both the physical security of the nation and its democratic values and institutions.

Yet not enough had been done as the danger posed by Nazi Germany to Great Britain, the Western Hemisphere, and the United States was greater than ever. "The blunt truth is this," Roosevelt warned. "The present rate of Nazi sinkings of merchant ships is more than three times as high as the capacity of British shipyards to replace them; it is more than twice the combined British and American output of merchant ships today." With the recent German victories in the Mediterranean, the Nazis now threatened to control all of northern Africa to Dakar and the "island outposts of the New World—the Azores and Cape Verde Islands." The war was now "approaching the brink of the Western Hemisphere itself. It is coming very close to home." What the president now termed the "Battle of the Atlantic" extended from the "icy waters of the North Pole to the frozen continent of the Antarctic."[20]

The lightning speed of modern warfare and the advances in weaponry demanded a reconsideration of the methods of national defense and the definition of national security. An attack, Roosevelt claimed, was not just the bombing of New York or San Francisco. A loss of the islands of the Atlantic or a German occupation of Iceland and Greenland "would directly endanger the freedom of the Atlantic and our own American physical safety." Anyone with an atlas could see the problem. "When the enemy comes at you in a tank or a bombing plane, if you hold your fire until you see the whites of his eyes, you will never know what hit you. Our Bunker Hill of tomorrow may be several thousand miles from Boston."[21] While the United States was not yet formally a belligerent, the "Battle of the Atlantic" and Roosevelt's declaration of a national emergency had brought it as close as possible without the actual firing of shots.

When Germany invaded the Soviet Union on June 22, it appeared to most observers that the fight would be a repeat of its blitzkrieg victory over France in 1940. As German forces rapidly advanced hundreds of miles into the Soviet Union, most senior U.S. officials thought that the Russian forces would collapse and that the Nazis would be victorious by the end of the summer. Given this, they saw little reason to send aid to the Soviet Union as it would either be wasted or fall into German hands. Roosevelt was not so sure. Unlike others, the president thought that the Soviet Union would hang on and that its ability to survive and fight the Germans would be decisive not only in relieving the pressure on Great Britain but also in defeating Germany. As Churchill, a man whose anticommunist beliefs were well known, told the British public in explaining why Britain would aid the Russians, Nazism and Bolshevism may be indistinguishable in many ways, but this was secondary to Great Britain's "single, irrevocable purpose . . . to destroy Hitler and every vestige of the Nazi regime."[22]

Roosevelt's thinking was similar to the British prime minister's. He worried that if aid was not sent to the Soviet Union and the Germans were victorious, one would always wonder if support might have made a difference. While the president was painfully aware of key supply shortages and had no desire to waste them, he saw the survival of the Soviet Union as crucial to an ultimate victory. Roosevelt's instincts were confirmed when he sent Harry Hopkins to Moscow in July to meet with Stalin and assess the Soviets' needs. Hopkins reported that Soviet resistance was stiffening, that the Soviets had the will to fight a long war, and that Russia would not fall that year. Based on this report and his own strategic calculus, Roosevelt ordered that aid, particularly airplanes, be sent immediately.

Right after issuing these orders, Roosevelt slipped away from Washington, D.C., for a secret meeting with Winston Churchill off the coast of Newfoundland. The conference from August 9–12 was the first of many summits between the two men and created the close bond that saw them and their nations through the war. The culmination of the meeting was the

Roosevelt signs the Lend-Lease Act, March 11, 1941.
Franklin D. Roosevelt Library

release of the "Atlantic Charter" on August 14. The eight points that made up the statement of war aims by the two English-speaking democracies reflected the essential elements of Roosevelt's internationalism: no territorial aggrandizement from war, self-determination for all nations, the open door policy for international trade, disarmament, and a permanent peace built upon international cooperation and adherence to these values.

The next day, Roosevelt and Churchill released an often-overlooked joint message to Stalin. They praised the Soviets for their "splendid defense" against the Nazi attack and noted that shiploads of supplies had already been sent with more to follow to aid Russia in its fight. The key point of the message was a request for a meeting in Moscow of senior officials to ascertain the Soviet Union's needs for manufactured goods, weapons, and raw materials to maximize the effectiveness of production planning and their use. The two leaders informed Stalin that if he approved the idea, the West would continue to send supplies as rapidly as possible until such a meeting. In conclusion, they set out their hope for wartime cooperation, noting "how vitally important to the defeat of Hitlerism is the brave and steadfast resistance of the Soviet Union" and the necessity for "planning the program for the future allocation of our joint resources." As the president noted in a press conference on August 16, all of this was based on the assumption that Russian resistance would continue into the winter.[23] From the German invasion of the Soviet Union and these considerations, the Grand Alliance of World War II was formed. Only Nazi aggression could have brought together the world's largest empire, leading capitalist nation, and only communist country into a working alliance that would ultimately triumph in World War II over the Axis.

Along with planning for extending aid to the Soviet Union, in September Roosevelt also took his final steps toward war with Germany. On September 4, a German submarine attacked the American destroyer *Greer* off the coast of Greenland. A week later, Roosevelt reported the attack to the American public in a fireside chat, telling them it was an unprovoked action against a ship carrying mail, and with the American flag clearly displayed, inside the zone in the Atlantic the United States claimed as its waters of self-defense. "This was piracy—piracy legally and morally," Roosevelt declared and consistent with German aggression elsewhere in the Atlantic. "The important truth is that these acts of international lawlessness are a manifestation of a . . . Nazi design to abolish the freedom of the seas, and to acquire absolute control and domination of these seas for themselves," all with the ultimate aim of the domination of the United States and the Western Hemisphere. The president pledged, "No matter what it takes, no matter what it costs, we will keep open the line of legitimate commerce in these defensive waters."[24]

The president did not tell the public that the *Greer*, along with British aircraft, had been following the sub for hours in hopes that the British could sink it. Rather, he compared the German submarine to a rattlesnake and noted that when it is "poised to strike, you do not wait until he has struck before you crush him." Given that, he announced what became called the policy of "shoot-on-sight." American naval vessels and planes would no longer wait for German subs to strike first but would attack if they found German ships inside the Atlantic defense sphere.[25]

Roosevelt and British prime minister Winston S. Churchill on board HMS Prince of Wales *on August 10, 1941, a summit that resulted in the Atlantic Charter.*
Franklin D. Roosevelt Library

The president, however, still did not seek a formal declaration of war. The main role of the United States, unless directly attacked, was to be the arsenal of democracy and to supply Great Britain and now the Soviet Union with the materials necessary for victory. The longer the United States stayed out, the quicker it could produce weapons and the stronger it would become. Moreover, with Japan's renewed aggression in Southeast Asia, Roosevelt worried about a two-front war, particularly before the nation had fully mobilized its productive power. The president had to be sure that his actions maintained public support and that his policies worked in conjunction toward the defeat of the Axis and not at cross-purposes. Thus, he was still following a policy of preparedness, support for the allies, and delay while America marshaled its resources for war.

For the past year, Roosevelt had been willing to take actions that were more and more hostile toward Germany, but he was determined to wait for the war to come to the United States. He continued to demonstrate the political acuity that had won him three terms in office and was moving the nation as fast as he thought was possible without harming his ultimate goal of defeating Nazi Germany and establishing internationalism as the basis of the nation's foreign policy. There remained considerable neutralist sentiment in Congress, and Roosevelt wanted to be sure that when war came there was no doubt as to who was the aggressor and that he had a unified nation behind him. Given the conviction of all senior officials that the German threat was much greater that that from Japan, that the decisive theater of the world crisis was Europe, and that America had to defeat Germany, it was somewhat surprising that, when war finally came to the United States, it came in the Pacific and not the Atlantic.

Pearl Harbor

Throughout 1940 and 1941, American efforts were concentrated primarily on Europe and the Nazi German threat. Great Britain's survival was still not certain, and if Germany defeated the Soviet Union, its military and industry would be greatly strengthened and it could turn its full attention again to the British Isles. Moreover, up to the middle of 1941, senior officials did not believe that Japan would be bold or foolish enough to provoke the United States, much less attack it. They were convinced that the United States had much greater power than Japan, that Japanese leaders knew this, and that any such action would be suicide by Tokyo. This did not mean that Japan was ignored: the Roosevelt administration had taken steps to deter further Japanese aggression and set out its determination to protect U.S. and Western interests in Southeast Asia. Shortly after Japan took advantage of Germany's victory over France in 1940 to move into northern Indochina, the American embargo of scrap metal and iron was felt by Japan's military and appeared to many American officials to serve as a sufficient deterrent. Tokyo had to use up reserves to sustain the fighting and renewed efforts to open up negotiations with Washington. As Stimson noted, summarizing American policy at the end of 1940, "when the United States indicates by clear language and bold actions that she intends to carry out a clear and affirmative policy in the Far East, Japan will yield to that policy even though it conflicts with her own Asiatic policy and conceived interests."[26]

Indeed, so sure were many American officials that Japan would never strike against the United States that they discussed removing the American fleet from Hawaii and the West Coast to the Atlantic in 1941 and believed that time was an ally in East Asia. In part, this confidence stemmed from the development of the B-17 bomber. The newest version of the Flying Fortress had a range great enough to strike Japan from the Philippines and, so thought many strategists, would provide a deterrent to any further Japanese expansion. At the end of 1940, therefore, policy was designed to preserve the status quo in the Pacific until the Allies' fortunes greatly improved in Europe.

Yet the status quo was hardly an ideal situation, or one that the United States wanted to see become permanent, and no one could confidently predict Japanese actions. Conflict at some point appeared inevitable. The question was whether or not it would be to U.S. advantage, if Japan renewed its expansion and pushed toward the south, to have, in the words of Ambassador Joseph Grew a "showdown sooner or to have it later." The answer to that question depended on whether war with Japan would harm the U.S. ability to aid Britain in Europe and thus make the difference between victory and defeat for England and when the American preparedness program reached the point where the United States could take on commitments in two oceans. Everyone, including Grew, the previous leader of the faction that urged a negotiated settlement, realized that the problem had no peaceful solution. Japan, the ambassador acknowledged in a letter to Roosevelt, was "openly and unashamedly one of the predatory nations and part of a system which aims to wreck about everything that the United States stands for." The remaining question then was, how much pressure should be applied? A full American embargo "will seriously handicap Japan in the long run" but could "push the Japanese onward in a forlorn hope of making themselves economically self-sufficient." As Grew concluded, it was "not whether we must call a halt to the Japanese program, but when."[27]

The president responded in January 1941 that he was in complete agreement with Grew. In deciding what course of action to take, it was imperative to understand "that the hostilities in Europe, in Africa, and in Asia are all parts of a single world conflict" that have forced the United States into "defending our way of life and our vital interests wherever they are seriously endangered." This demanded a global strategy that measured all steps by what was best and necessary to defeat Germany. Thus, it was not just a question of whether war with Japan would divert American resources away from helping Great Britain. It was also necessary to "consider whether, if Japan should gain possession of the region of the Netherlands East Indies and the Malay Peninsula, the chances of England's winning in her struggle with Germany would not be decreased thereby." The resources of the area and British access to them were also vital to the war effort. "Our strategy of giving them assistance toward ensuring our own security must envisage both sending of supplies to England and helping to prevent a closing of the channels of communication to and from various parts of the world, so that other important sources of supply will not be denied to the British and added to the assets of the other side." The problems Japan posed were so interrelated with the war in Europe, Roosevelt concluded, that "any attempt to state them compels one to think in terms of five continents and seven seas."[28]

Starting in February 1941, Japan's new ambassador to the United States, Admiral Nomura Kichisaburô, engaged in a series of talks with Secretary of State Cordell Hull to find some ground for an American accommodation to Japan's domination of China and imperial project. Nomura represented the moderate faction in the Japanese government that still sought a modus vivendi with the United States in the hope that Japan could secure its goals without war. The Japanese position that the United States should accept Japan's dominate position in East Asia, however, was untenable to the Roosevelt administration, and the talks went nowhere that winter and spring. The United States was content at this time to drag the talks out and thus buy time for its mobilization and allow it to focus on getting aid to Great Britain.

The events of July 1941 completely changed these views. Japan's taking of all of Indochina indicated that Tokyo's effort to establish its dominance throughout East Asia could not be stopped with methods short of war. Moreover, the German invasion of the Soviet Union the month before had changed the strategic equation in Europe and confirmed for President Roosevelt his view that the fighting was all one world war that demanded a coordinated American response to the international crisis. In particular, Roosevelt worried that a Japanese attack against the Soviet Union might tilt the balance and lead to Moscow's defeat. If war with Japan was to come, it had to be in Southeast Asia, where the United States was stronger and the battles would not so dramatically change the fortunes of the war against Hitler. The need to ensure the Soviet Union's survival, as the president saw it, necessitated taking a firmer position and greater risks in U.S. policy toward Japan and a willingness to take steps that risked war in the Pacific rather than just a policy of deterrence. This was not a reversal of the view that American resources had to be concentrated in Europe because Germany was the greater threat; rather it was consistent with this strategy as the Soviet Union was now the key piece in the effort to defeat the Nazis.[29]

On July 26, Roosevelt announced that he was freezing Japanese assets in the United States, a move that in effect became an oil embargo against Japan. Explaining his thinking to the public that day, the president noted, "There is a world war going on, and has been for some time—nearly two years." One of Washington's goals had been to prevent the fighting from spreading to new areas, notably the rest of Indochina, the Dutch East Indies, and the South Pacific. This was necessary to keep open a line of vital supplies going to Europe. "Now, if we cut the oil off, they probably would have gone down to the Dutch East Indies a year ago, and you would have had war." Without saying so, the president had indicated that his thinking had changed and he was now willing to risk that war.[30]

The freezing of Japan's assets and the oil embargo led Nomura to start another round of talks designed to improve relations in mid-August. The Japanese promised to guarantee the Philippines' integrity and withdraw their forces from Southeast Asia and the southwestern Pacific pending an agreement by the United States to cease sending aid to China. In return the United States would lift its embargo and normalize relations with Japan. Not surprising, the State Department rejected this, along with the proposal for a meeting between President Roosevelt and Japanese prime minister Fumimaro Konoe. The administration's position was that relations would improve only when Japan acknowledged its respect for China's sovereignty and territorial integrity, the open door, and nonaggression.[31]

As talks went nowhere that fall, the War Department began preparing for the Philippines' defense and the coming of war. Stimson told Hull he would need three months to secure American defenses in the Pacific and, therefore, favored a continuation of the efforts at "stringing out negotiations during that time." In mid-October, he noted that it was important that American "diplomatic fencing" be conducted in such a way "so as to be sure that Japan was put into the wrong and made the first bad move—overt move." Hull asked Stimson if he favored an immediate declaration of war. The secretary of war emphatically responded no. The United States needed "to take advantage of this wonderful opportunity of strengthening our position in the Philippines by air." Hull, because he thought the Japanese emperor favored a peaceful settlement, still thought negotiation could succeed. He was alone at the top of the administration in thinking this. Nonetheless, Stimson, while convinced that war was now a foregone conclusion and reflecting Roosevelt's views, encouraged Hull to continue the talks as long as possible as the buildup of American forces could only strengthen the diplomatic efforts and delay the war's start. Stimson summed up his position by quoting Theodore Roosevelt: The U.S. policy was to "speak softly and carry a big stick." What was needed was a little more time to get the stick prepared.[32]

By late November, it was clear that time was quickly running out. The final Japanese offer on November 20 of a withdrawal from Indochina in return for a lifting of U.S. sanctions was rejected, as was the U.S. counteroffer of a Japanese agreement to leave China in return for talks and trade. The United States had broken the Japanese diplomatic code, and Washington knew that this final breakdown of talks meant war. It was now just a matter of when and where. In a meeting of senior administration officials on November 25, all concurred that a Japanese attack was likely and that it would come without warning. "The question was how we should maneuver them into the position of firing the first shot without allowing too much danger to ourselves." This would make it clear that Japan was the aggressor in the war to be fought.[33] On December 1, the Japanese Imperial Conference concluded that there was no turning back and gave the green light for the attack on Pearl Harbor.

The Roosevelt administration believed that Japan would strike to the south, at the Dutch East Indies, Malaysia, and possibly the Philippines, to remove the American and British navies from the area and gain access to the region's riches, particularly oil. Washington was shocked when on

Roosevelt signs the declaration of war against Japan, December 8, 1941.
Franklin D. Roosevelt Library

December 7 the attack came on Pearl Harbor in Hawaii. Although the initial reports from the islands were bad, there was a sense of relief in the nation's capital as the indecision and anticipation of war was over, and as Stimson put it, because of the Japanese attack, the war "had come in a way which would unite all our people."[34] The nation agreed with Roosevelt when he declared that December 7 was a "date which will live in infamy."[35]

This is not to discount the concern over the failure at Pearl Harbor or the damage inflicted, but to acknowledge what the president had concluded that fall; to protect American interests, the United States had not only to provide aid to its allies and prepare its defenses but also to become a belligerent itself so as to ensure victory during the war and to seize the second chance at achieving victory after the war as well.

Almost immediately, charges were made that the Roosevelt administration had conspired to set up the attack on Pearl Harbor as a way to overcome the noninterventionist sentiment in the nation and as a back door to the war in Europe that the people would not support otherwise. These charges are serious and completely wrong. It is true that the president and his senior advisers knew that the rejection of Japan's final negotiation proposal meant war, that they had long been frustrated by political opposition at home and the desire of so many to stay out of the fighting at seemingly any cost, and that they wanted Japan and/or Germany to make the first overt attack to clarify the issue of who the aggressor was and to unite the nation in combat.

Still, there is no evidence to support the claim that the Roosevelt administration manipulated Japan into war and that the president left the Pacific fleet open to the devastating attack on Pearl Harbor on purpose and in the process hampered the American ability to defend against the Japanese strikes in the southern Pacific. Officials in Washington were genuinely surprised by the attack. The United States had broken Japan's diplomatic code, not its military code, and it did not have prior knowledge of the specifics of Japan's war plan. Administration officials assumed that Japan would strike to the south, at Malaysia, the Dutch East Indies, and the Philippines, which it did in addition to the attack on Hawaii. The attack on Pearl Harbor resulted in part from Washington's underestimates of the Japanese military's capabilities and from its failure to consider that Japan would strike other areas along with Southeast Asia when it decided to attack. Local commanders shared this misperception and, as Stimson noted, failed to act fully on the alert sent out from Washington to all officers and bases in the Pacific to be prepared for war. The credit for the surprise must go to the Japanese who planned and carried it out, exploiting the misperceptions of American officials with their daring move.

Furthermore, despite Stimson's urging, Roosevelt did not ask for a declaration of war on Germany after the attack on Pearl Harbor, even though all senior officials agreed that the Nazis posed the greater threat to the United States. It is impossible to know what Roosevelt would have done had Germany not decided on December 11 to declare war on the United States. The attack on Pearl Harbor had overcome all resistance to war at home, but the public wanted to fight Japan, not Germany. Still, there probably would have been an incident in the Atlantic that would have brought about hostilities. Roosevelt had always made much of the Axis alliance, even if the Tri-Partite Pact did not mean much, as he saw the fighting as one world war, with the events and consequences for the United States linked.

CONCLUSION

FOR THOSE FAMILIAR WITH AMERICAN FOREIGN POLICY during the Cold War, Roosevelt's views during the late 1930s and early 1940s and his justification for American involvement in World War II might not seem too notable or unique. They became the basis for American foreign policy during the war and in the postwar period. Yet, at the time, with few exceptions, Roosevelt was out in front in making the case for an active American opposition to German, Japanese, and Italian aggression. In the span of four years, Franklin Roosevelt carried out what he saw as his education of the American people about the danger aggressor nations posed to the United States, its real interests in the world, and the need to adopt and support an internationalist foreign policy. It was a gradual process, moving from setting out the parameters of American interests and the just war doctrine in his Quarantine Speech to modifications in the neutrality laws, aid to the Allies, and finally war itself. The period between June 1940 and the passage of the Lend-Lease Act was the critical time when the nation embraced Roosevelt's understanding of the crisis and the proper role of the United States as a great power and took the steps that led to its participation in World War II.

Yet the seeds for Roosevelt's success go back further than 1937, to his first term in office, when he embraced the Stimson Doctrine as the American position on aggression, established the Good Neighbor policy that created hemispheric unity, and began searching for a solution to the emerging crisis in Europe. Throughout the decade, the president maintained his commitment to internationalism, and events proved that he had been

correct on the major issues confronting the nation. Moreover, he had prepared the nation well for World War II's trials by securing the foundation
for the buildup of the American military through the draft, mobilization of
the economy, and the massive effort to produce the weapons of war.
Roosevelt's gradual approach to the crisis meant that when war came the
American people were ready for the sacrifices necessary for victory over
Germany and Japan and willing to take up the position and responsibility of
being the leading power in the world.

There was nothing inevitable about this remarkable achievement.
While the nation was never isolationist, in that it sought to cut itself off
from the world, a large majority of Americans throughout the 1930s favored neutrality legislation and wanted the nation to stay out of any wars
outside of the Western Hemisphere. The negative views of World War I,
its failed peace, and the economic crisis at the end of the 1920s were
firmly entrenched and could not be easily changed. In moving cautiously at
first and then with more determination in 1940 and 1941, Roosevelt was
able to confront the logic and arguments of the anti-interventionists without ever losing his popularity. By casting his policies as necessary for the
defense of America against an irrational and evil enemy, he also framed
them as morally correct, necessary to maintain the nation's democratic
institutions and values, and, therefore, just actions in the face of international aggression and lawlessness. Roosevelt thus redefined U.S. national
security as global in scope and best secured through an active foreign policy
that pursued cooperation with allies, collective security, and the promotion
of American interests and values abroad. The years leading up to World
War II, therefore, were the defining and decisive moment of change in
American foreign policy and continue to influence the nation's interactions
with the world today.

In February 1941, Henry Luce, the publisher of *Time*, *Life*, and *Fortune*
magazines, captured the logic behind much of the internationalist position
on foreign policy; the emerging, confident mood of the nation; and its
highest aspirations in his essay "The American Century." Luce argued that
the failure of the United States to accept its responsibility as a great power
and take up the position of world leader during the interwar period "had
disastrous consequences" for the nation "and for all mankind." A permanent peace and continuous prosperity could be secured only through the
establishment of the "American Century," during which the United States
would take up its rightful role and responsibilities. As Luce explained the

recent past, he asserted that in 1919 the United States missed "a golden opportunity . . . to assume the leadership of the world. . . . We did not understand the opportunity. [President Woodrow] Wilson mishandled it. We rejected it." The result was the Great Depression and a second world war. To avoid repeating the same mistake with the same consequences this time, the United States had to seize the second chance presented to it to lead the world. "It is for America and America alone to determine," Luce declared, "whether a system of free enterprise—an economic order compatible with freedom and progress—shall or shall not prevail in this country. We know perfectly well that there is not the slightest chance of anything faintly resembling a free enterprise system prevailing in this country if it prevails nowhere else." If the United States did not establish such a system internationally, then economic disruption and political chaos would return. Stating the central ideas that all leading American internationalists held to, Luce argued that it was essential that the United States promote American ideals of freedom, justice, and opportunity to make sure they spread throughout the world. "America as the dynamic center of ever-widening spheres of enterprise," Luce declared, "America as the training center of the skilled servants of mankind, America as the Good Samaritan, really believing again that it is more blessed to give than to receive, and America as the powerhouse of the ideals of Freedom and Justice—out of these elements surely can be fashioned a vision of the 20th Century to which we can and will devote ourselves." In this spirit, Luce concluded, the United States was called to "create the first great American Century."[1]

The war brought the nation out of the Great Depression at home and restored prosperity and confidence. But it was also seen as a second chance for the United States to create a lasting peace, one based on American interests and values. For American leaders and the American people, the war as not just a defensive effort to defeat German and Japanese aggression but also a battle to destroy the evil these countries represented and to reshape the world in the U.S. image. The extent of Roosevelt's achievement is evident in Luce's statement of America's wartime goals and in Americans' memories of World War II. Franklin D. Roosevelt's use of just war arguments and fighting for values such as the four freedoms explains why World War II was seen as the "Good War" by so many Americans when it was fought and after.[2]

APPENDIX OF
DOCUMENTS

The Good Neighbor Policy and Latin America

1. The Clark Memorandum Refutes the Roosevelt
Corollary to the Monroe Doctrine

Source: U.S. Department of State, *Memorandum on the Monroe Doctrine Prepared by J. Rueben Clark, Undersecretary of State, 17 December 1928* (Washington, DC: Government Printing Office, 1930).

In his annual message to Congress on December 6, 1904, President Theodore Roosevelt announced the Roosevelt Corollary to the Monroe Doctrine. He claimed that the United States, in adherence to the obligations of the Monroe Doctrine, had the right to intervene in other nations in the Western Hemisphere to maintain order. With protests growing in Latin America over unilateral interventions by the United States, Secretary of State Frank B. Kellogg asked J. Rueben Clark to study the legality of the Roosevelt Corollary. Written in December 1928, it was not published until 1930 by Secretary of State Henry L. Stimson.

It is of first importance to have in mind that Monroe's declaration in its terms, relates solely to the relationships between European states on the one side, and, on the other side, the American continents. . . .

Nor does the declaration purport to lay down any principles that are to govern the interrelationship of the states of this Western Hemisphere as among themselves.

The Doctrine states a case of United States vs. Europe, not of United States vs. Latin America.

Such arrangements as the United States has made, for example, with Cuba, Santo Domingo, Haiti, and Nicaragua, are not within the Doctrine as it was announced by Monroe. . . .

Should it become necessary to apply a sanction for a violation of the Doctrine as declared by Monroe, that sanction would run against the European power offending the policy, and not against the Latin American country which was the object of the European aggression. . . .

In the normal case, the Latin American state against which aggression was aimed by a European power, would be the beneficiary of the Doctrine not its victim. This has been the history of its application. The Doctrine makes the United States a guarantor, in effect, of the independence of Latin American states. . . .

The so-called "Roosevelt Corollary" was to the effect . . . that in case of financial or other difficulties in weak Latin American countries, the United States should attempt an adjustment thereof lest European Governments should intervene, and intervening should occupy territory—an act which would contrary to the principles of the Monroe Doctrine. . . . As has already been indicated above, it is not believed that this corollary is justified by the terms of the Monroe Doctrine, however much it may be justified by the application of the doctrine of self-preservation. . . .

2. President Franklin D. Roosevelt on the
Good Neighbor Policy

Source: Samuel I. Rosenman, ed., *The Public Papers and Addresses of Franklin D. Roosevelt* (New York: Random House, 1941), vol. 2, 129–33; and Edgar B. Nixon, ed., *Franklin D. Roosevelt and Foreign Affairs* (Cambridge, MA: Belknap Press of Harvard University Press, 1969), vol. 1, 558–63.

The excerpts below come from two speeches President Roosevelt made during his first year in office, on April 12, 1933, before the Governing Board of the Pan American Union in Washington, D.C., in celebration of "Pan-American Day" and on December 28, 1933, at the Woodrow Wilson Foundation Dinner in Washington, D.C. In both speeches, the president's internationalist view is evident, as are the contrasts he will make later in the decade with the policies of the Axis nations.

April 12, 1933

In my Inaugural Address I stated that I would "dedicate this Nation to the policy of the good neighbor—the neighbor who resolutely respects himself and, because he does so, respects the rights of other—the neighbor who respects his obligation and respects the sanctity of his agreements in and with a world of neighbors." Never before has the significance of the words "good neighbor" been so manifest in international relations. . . .

The essential qualities of a true pan Americanism must be the same as those which constitute a good neighbor, namely, mutual understanding, and through such understanding, a sympathetic appreciation of the other's point of view. . . . In this spirit the people of every Republic on our continent are coming to a deep understanding of the fact that the Monroe Doctrine . . . was and is directed at the maintenance of independence by the peoples of the continent. It was aimed and is aimed against the acquisition in any manner of the control of additional territory in this hemisphere by any non-American power.

December 28, 1933

I do not hesitate to say that if I had . . . been engaged in a political campaign as a citizen of some other American republic I might have been strongly tempted to play upon the fears of my compatriots of the republic by charging the United States of North America with some form of imperialistic desire for selfish aggrandizement. . . . I might have found it difficult to believe fully in the altruism of the richest American republic. In particular . . . I might have found it hard to approve of the occupation of territory of other republics, even as a temporary measure. . . .

It therefore has seemed clear to me as President that the time has come to . . . [state] that the definite policy of the United States from now on is one opposed to armed intervention.

The Stimson Doctrine and Relations With Japan to 1939

3. The Stimson Doctrine

Source: U.S. Department of State, *Foreign Relations of the United States: Japan, 1931–1941* (Washington, DC: Government Printing Office, 1943), vol. 1, 76.

On January 7, 1932, Secretary of State Henry L. Stimson issued the Stimson Doc-

trine in response to the Japanese invasion of Manchuria on September 18, 1931.
Stimson's policy of nonrecognition continued until the outbreak of World War II.

With the recent [Japanese] military operations about Chinchow, the last remaining administrative authority of the Government of the Chinese Republic in South Manchuria, as it existed prior to September 18th, 1931, has been destroyed. . . . In view of the present situation and of its own rights and obligations therein, the American government deems it to be its duty to notify both the Imperial Japanese Government and the Government of the Chinese Republic that it cannot admit the legality of any situation *de facto* nor does it intend to recognize any treaty or agreement entered into between those Governments . . . which may impair the treaty rights of the United States or its citizens in China, including those which relate to the sovereignty, the independence, or the territorial and administrative integrity of the Republic of China, or to the international policy relative to China, commonly known as the open door policy.

4. Ambassador Joseph Grew Sets Out the Problems in Relations With Japan

Source: Joseph Grew to Cordell Hull, May 11, 1933, and February 6, 1935, President's Secretary File: Japan, Box 42, Franklin D. Roosevelt Presidential Library, Hyde Park, NY.

Early in President Roosevelt's first term in office, Ambassador to Japan Joseph Grew explained the extent of the problems the United States faced in relations with Japan in a letter of May 11, 1933, to Secretary of State Cordell Hull. Grew saw Japan's military potential and tried to explain the logic of expansion that guided many Japanese officials. Two years later, in another letter to Hull, Grew set out to explain how the Japanese understood their position in the world, to see the picture "through the eyes of the Japanese themselves," and why this was leading to an "urge toward expansion in Japan."

May 11, 1933
I would like to describe to you, briefly, the whole picture as I see it; that is, the strength of the Japanese nation as a whole and particularly the strength of the combined Japanese fighting machine. Japan is so often spoken of as a small, overcrowded nation, cooped up within the confines of a few small islands, without natural resources, and largely dependent upon foreign sources

for its foodstuffs, that people in other countries sometimes fail to appreciate the facts and to realize the actual and potential power of these people.

The Japanese Empire is not a small country, as compared with the countries of Europe, at least. The Empire itself . . . including the area of "Manchukuo", which to all practical purposes is under Japanese control, . . . is greater than that of France, Germany, Spain, Switzerland, Belgium, Netherlands and Denmark combined. The population of the Japanese Empire proper is 90 million; with that of "Manchukuo" it is around 120 million, or nearly the same as that of the United States. And these people (or that part of them which is of the Japanese race) are intelligent, industrious, energetic, extremely nationalistic, war-loving, aggressive and, it must be admitted, somewhat unscrupulous. So Japan cannot be considered a small or weak country. . . . Moreover, the nation has developed its industries in recent years until it is able to supply itself with all of the necessities of life, and can build all the ships, and make all the airplanes, tanks, guns, ammunition, chemicals, etc., needed to wage a severe war, if it is not too protracted. Furthermore, it has large reserves of war materials, such as petroleum, nitrates, etc., not produced within the country. . . .

Turning to the armed forces of the country, it is my opinion that Japan probably has the most complete, well-balanced, co-ordinated and therefore powerful fighting machine in the world today. . . . The Japanese fighting machine, unless I am very much mistaken, is designed for the purpose of keeping Western nations from interfering while Japan carries out its ambitions in Asia. . . . It is true that the Japanese fighting forces consider the United States as their potential enemy . . . because they think that the United States is standing in the path of the nation's natural expansion and is more apt to interfere with Japan's ambitions than are the European nations. . . .

More than the size of the nation or the strength of its fighting machine, however, the thing which makes the Japanese nation actually so powerful and potentially so menacing, is the national morale and esprit de corps—a spirit which perhaps has not been equalled [sic] since the days when the Mongol hordes followed Genghis Khan in his conquest of Asia. The force of a nation bound together with great moral determination, fired with national ambition, and peopled by a race with unbounded capacity for courageous self-sacrifice is not easy to overestimate.

February 6, 1935

The general conclusion drawn is that there exists in Japan today a definite urge toward economic and political expansion in East Asia and, as a corollary, a growing pressure against the interests of western nations, including the interests of the United States, in this part of the world. . . .

Psychologically, the Japanese resent being considered on a different footing from other nations. They believe they occupy a position which entitles them to the same consideration in the Far East that the British and French claim in the affairs of Europe or even the United States in the Western Hemisphere, and they intend to assert and maintain this position with all the strength at their command.

In addition, or perhaps at the back of this attitude, is the expansionist urge due to the economic problem involved in the struggle for existence, the normal tendency and striving to achieve a higher standard of living and the acute competition inevitably arising therefrom. To a certain extent the Japanese are a revolutionary force in the Far East. They feel that the Western Powers have exploited China with little benefit to the Chinese; that there must be an end to this activity and that Japan is called to act. Besides, the Japanese believe that it will be profitable. With a larger sphere of activity Japanese industry and commerce will expand further and remove the spectre of restricted markets from their eyes. If this has to be done at others' expense it cannot be helped. There is in the Japanese attitude something of the "manifest destiny" idea, or the point of view expressed by Kipling in his poems of the British Empire.

It therefore behooves us to examine this expansionist urge in Japan as the reasonable and logical operation of well-nigh irrepressible forces based on the underlying principle of self preservation. We are apt to stress the military aspects of Japanese activity without carefully considering the driving impulse of the whole nation. If, from an examination of concrete evidence, we became convinced that Japan is faced with a national problem of the utmost gravity brought about primarily by natural developments, and that military covetousness is only one phase or expression of it, and if we furthermore become convinced that failing certain outlets which will act as safety valve, some sort of explosion or series of explosions along the lines of the Manchurian affair must inevitably occur, we may pause to consider the wisdom of basing our own policy toward Japan on two concurrent principles: (1) national preparedness for the purpose of protecting our legitimate interests in the Far East, and at the same time (2) a sympathetic, cooperative and helpful attitude toward Japan, based on larger considerations reaching into the future. . . .

The Japanese see themselves as an overpopulated nation, but as a nation of active, intelligent and progressive people, anxious to find a "place in the sun," and to raise their standard of living. At the same time they see themselves as badly handicapped by limited workable natural resources and by a lack of economic opportunity within the territories which they control. . . .

The satisfaction of Japanese needs will require, primarily, more economic elbow-room for the nation. . . . They can, as in the past, do this by means of military force, but further Japanese military adventures in the Far East would very probably result in a tremendous clash with the Western powers. . . . The problem confronting Western nations, therefore, when reduced to its simplest terms, would appear to be whether to endeavor to preserve Western interests in the Far East for a generation or two by defeating Japan in a war, or whether to endeavor to satisfy Japan's urge for economic expansion by granting larger markets and greater opportunity for Japanese enterprise in the territories controlled by the Western nations.

5. Stanley Hornbeck, Chief of the Division of Far Eastern Affairs, Calls for American Preparedness Against Japan, March 27, 1935

Source: *FRUS, 1935*, vol. 3, 855–57.

Hornbeck, unlike Grew, saw no room for compromise with Japan and was one of the first officials in the Roosevelt administration who sought to build upon the Stimson Doctrine to make a policy of opposition toward all aspects of Japanese expansion. In the following memorandum, Hornbeck was the first State Department official to call for military preparedness against Japan.

The fundamental concepts of nations do not change rapidly. The concepts and the objectives of the Japanese being what they are today, and their mental and physical vigor being what they are, and their morale being what it is, there is substantial likelihood that, barring unpredictable political accidents or acts of God, the time will come within the next few years when the Japanese people will feel strongly moved to defy the United States and cross swords with us. At such a moment, the only thing which would deter them would be the conviction on the part of those persons who have ultimate authority in Japan that Japan would have no chance of success and would be doomed to decisive defeat if the trial were made.

For that reason, the best chance for peace as between the United States and Japan must lie in the possession by the United States of machinery of military defense strong enough to deter the Japanese from daring to attack.

No conceivable concessions on the part of the Government and people of the United States would have any conclusive effect in regard to this problem. . . .

It is absolutely essential that we take stock of Japan today as Japan is.

The *politik* of force—a manifestation and instrument of imperialism rampant—upon which Japan relies and will increasingly rely can be dealt with effectively insofar as the problem of national security of other nations is concerned only by imposing obstacles or the interposition of force. The people of the United States are in possession of intellectual and material resources such that they can create the obstacles or the instruments of force which are, more and more, imperatively called for in this situation. The American Government should see to it that these resources are adequately employed toward those ends.

This country is not going to embark upon any aggression against Japan. There can be no absolute assurance that Japan will not embark upon any aggression against us. But the likelihood of there being aggression and, in consequence, war will be diminished by, and only by, preparedness on our part of such nature and proportions as will tend definitely to discourage adventuring by Japan into acts of aggression against the United States.

6. President Franklin D. Roosevelt's Quarantine Speech

Source: Donald B. Schewe, ed., *Franklin D. Roosevelt and Foreign Affairs, January 1937–August 1939* (New York: Garland Press, 1979), vol. 7, doc. 530.

President Roosevelt, responding to Japan's full-scale invasion of China, announced in a October 5, 1937, speech in Chicago that aggressor nations should be "quarantined" by the peace-loving nations of the world to contain the threat. While never specifically mentioning Japan, and offering no specific policies, the president was making a case for aid to China. Moreover, he was beginning his campaign to educate the American people to the dangers abroad while setting out his internationalist perspective and case for a just war.

It is because the people of the United States under modern conditions must, for the sake of their own future, give thought to the rest of the world, that I, as the responsible executive head of the Nation, have chosen this great inland city . . . to speak to you on a subject of definite national importance.

The political situation in the world, which of late has been growing progressively worse, is such as to cause grave concern and anxiety to all the peoples and nations who wish to live in peace and amity with their neighbors.

Some fifteen years ago the hopes of mankind for a continuing era of international peace were raised to great heights when more that sixty nations solemnly pledged themselves not to resort to arms in furtherance of their national aims and policies. The high aspirations expressed in the Briand-Kellogg Peace Pact and the hopes for peace thus raised have of late given way to a haunting fear of calamity. The present reign of terror and international lawlessness began a few years ago.

It began through unjustified interference in the internal affairs of other nations or the invasion of alien territory in violation of treaties; and has now reached a stage where the very foundations of civilization are seriously threatened. The landmarks and traditions which have marked the progress of civilization towards a condition of law, order and justice and being wiped away.

Without a declaration of war and without warning of justification of any kind civilians, including women and children, are being ruthlessly murdered with bombs from the air. In times of so-called peace ships are being attacked and sunk by submarines without cause or notice. Nations are fomenting and taking sides in civil warfare in nations that have never done them any harm. Nations claiming freedom for themselves deny it to others.

Innocent peoples and nations are being cruelly sacrificed to a greed for power and supremacy which is devoid of all sense of justice and humane consideration. . . .

Let no one imagine that America will escape, that it may expect mercy, that this Western Hemisphere will not be attacked and that it will continue tranquilly and peacefully to carry on the ethics and the arts of civilization. . . .

The peace-loving nations must make a concerted effort in opposition to those violations of treaties and those ignorings of humane instincts which today are creating a state of international anarchy and instability from which there is no escape through mere isolation or neutrality.

Those who cherish their freedom and recognize and respect the equal right of their neighbors to be free and live in peace, must work together for the triumph of law and moral principles in order that peace, justice and confidence may prevail in the world. There must be a return to a belief in the pledged word in the value of a signed treaty. There must be recognition of the fact that national morality is as vital as private morality. . . .

There is a solidarity and interdependence about the modern world, both technically and morally, which makes it impossible for any nation completely to isolate itself from economic and political upheavals in the rest of the world, especially when such upheavals appear to be spreading and not declining. There can be no stability or peace either within nations or between nations except under laws and moral standards adhered to by all. International anarchy destroys every foundation for peace. It jeopardizes either the immediate or the future security of every nation, large or small. It is, therefore, a matter of vital interest and concern to the people of the United States that the sanctity of international treaties and the maintenance of international morality be restored.

The overwhelming majority of the peoples and nations of the world today want to live in peace. They seek the removal of barriers against trade. They want to exert themselves in industry, in agriculture and in business, that they may increase their wealth through the production of wealth-producing goods rather than striving to produce military planes and bombs and machine guns and cannon for the destruction of human lives and useful property.

In those nations of the world which seem to be piling armament on armament for purposes of aggression, and those other nations which fear acts of aggression against them and their security, a very high proportion of their national income is being spent directly for armaments. It runs from thirty to as high as fifty per cent.

The proportion that we in the United States spend is far less—eleven or twelve per cent.

How happy we are that the circumstances of the moment permit us to put our money into bridges and boulevards, dams and reforestations, the conservation of our soil and many other kinds of useful works rather than into huge standing armies and vast supplies of implements of war.

I am compelled and you are compelled, nevertheless, to look ahead. The peace, the freedom and the security of ninety per cent of the population of the world is being jeopardized by the remaining ten per cent who are threatening a breakdown of all international order and law. Surely the ninety per cent who want to live in peace under law and in accordance with moral standards that have received almost universal acceptance through the centuries, can and must find some way to make their will prevail.

The situation is definitely of universal concern. The questions involved relate not merely to violations of specific provisions of particular treaties: they are questions of war and of peace, of international law and especially of principles of humanity. . . .

It is true that the moral consciousness of the world must recognize the importance of removing injustices and well-founded grievances; but at the same time it must be aroused to the cardinal necessity of honoring the sanctity of treaties, of respecting the rights and liberties of others and of putting an end to acts of international aggression.

It seems to be unfortunately true that the epidemic of world lawlessness is spreading.

When an epidemic of physical disease starts to spread, the community approves and joins in a quarantine of the patients in order to protect the health of the community against the spread of the disease.

It is my determination to pursue a policy of peace and to adopt every practicable measure to avoid involvement in war. It ought to be inconceivable that in this modern era, and in the face of experience, any nation could be so foolish and ruthless as to run the risk of plunging the whole world into war by invading and violating, in contravention of solemn treaties, the territory of other nations that have done them no real harm and which are too weak to protect themselves adequately. Yet the peace of the world and the welfare and security of every nation is today being threatened by that very thing. . . .

War is a contagion, whether it be declared or undeclared. It can engulf states and peoples remote from the original scene of hostilities. We are determined to keep out of war, yet we cannot insure ourselves against the disastrous effects of war and the dangers of involvement. We are adopting such measures as will minimize our risk of involvement but we cannot have complete protection in a world of disorder in which confidence and security have broken down.

If civilization is to survive the principles of the Prince of Peace must be restored. Shattered trust between nations must be revived. . . .

America hates war. America hopes for peace. Therefore, America actively engages in the search for peace.

7. President Roosevelt Asks Congress for Increased Spending on Armaments, January 28, 1938

Source: Schewe, *Franklin D. Roosevelt and Foreign Affairs*, vol. 8., doc. 792.

On January 28, 1938, President Roosevelt made his first major request for larger military appropriations, asking for over $32 million in new spending along with a 20 percent increase in the existing authorized naval building program, two new battleships, and two new cruisers. In doing so, the president first set out his argument that the proper defense of the United States extended outside of the Western Hemisphere.

The Congress knows that for many years this Government has sought in many capitals with the leaders of many Governments to find a way to limit and reduce armaments and to establish at least the probability of world peace. . . .

We, as a peaceful Nation, cannot and will not abandon active search for an agreement among the nations to limit armaments and end aggression. But it is clear that until such agreement is reached—and I have not given up hope for it—we are compelled to think of our own national safety.

It is with the deepest regret that I report to you that armaments increase today at an unprecedented and alarming rate. It is an ominous fact that at least one-fourth of the world's population is involved in merciless devastating conflict in spite of the fact that most people in most countries, including those where conflict rages, wish to live at peace. Armies are fighting in the Far East and in Europe; thousands of civilians are being driven from their homes and bombed from the air. Tension throughout the world is high.

As Commander-in-Chief of the Army and Navy of the United States it is my constitutional duty to report to the Congress that our national defense is, in the light of increasing armaments of other Nations, inadequate for purposes of national security and requires increase for that purpose. . . .

It is necessary for all of us to realize that the unfortunate world condition today has resulted too often in the discarding of those principles and treaties which underlie law and order; and in the entrance of many new factors into the actual conduct of war.

Adequate defense means that for the protection not only of our coasts but also of our communities far removed from the coast, we must keep any potential enemy many hundred miles away from our continental limits.

We cannot assume that our defense would be limited to one ocean and one coast and that the other ocean and the other coast would with certainly be safe. We cannot be certain that the connecting link—the Panama Canal—would be safe. Adequate defense affects therefore the simultaneous defense of every part of the United States of America.

It is our clear duty to further every effort toward peace but at the same time to protect our Nation. That is the purpose of these recommendations. Such protection is and will be based not on aggression but on defense.

8. Japanese Foreign Minister Fumimaro Konoe Announces Japan's Claim to a "New Order in East Asia"

Source: *FRUS: Japan, 1931–1941*, vol. 1, 478.

On November 3, 1938, Tokyo proclaimed its intention to incorporate China in a new political order to formally establish Japan's control over that nation. With further expansion at the end of the decade, this new order later became the Greater East Asian Co-Prosperity Sphere, Japan's vision of its empire during World War II.

What Japan seeks is the establishment of a new order which will insure the permanent stability of East Asia. In this lies the ultimate purpose of our present military campaign [in China].

This new order has for its foundation a tripartite relationship of mutual aid and co-ordination between Japan, Manchoukuo and China in political, economic, cultural and other fields. Its object is to secure international justice, to perfect the joint defence against Communism, and to create a new culture and realize a close economic cohesion throughout East Asia. This indeed is the way to contribute toward the stabilization of East Asia and the progress of the world.

What Japan desires of China is that that country will share in the task of bringing about this new order in East Asia. She confidently expects that the people of China will fully comprehend her true intentions and that they will respond to the call of Japan for their co-operation. . . .

9. Stanley K. Hornbeck Calls for Economic Sanctions Against Japan, November 14, 1938

Source: Schewe, *Franklin D. Roosevelt and Foreign Affairs*, vol. 12, doc. 1403a.

Hornbeck, then the senior adviser on political relations in the State Department, worried that the lack of an effective American response to Japan's war in China had emboldened Tokyo and made Japanese expansion likely. The proclamation of Japan's new order confirmed this fear. He therefore called for a coordinated strategy, including economic sanctions, against Japan to deter Tokyo from further expansion and to hamper its ability to wage war.

It is an important interest of the United States that Japan not gain control of China. It therefore would be to our interest that Chinese resistance to Japan's efforts to gain that control continue. The Japanese nation today is animated by concepts and is pursuing objectives which are in conflict with the concepts and the legitimate objectives of the people of the United States. The Japanese are embarked upon a program of predatory imperialism. Unless the Japanese march is halted by the Chinese or by some other nation, the time will come when Japan and the United States will be face to face and definitely opposed to each other in the international political arena. It is desirable that the development of such a situation be prevented. It therefore is desirable that the United States act toward the preventing of such a development.

The American Government should formulate and adopt a program of action (a diplomatic "war plan") toward averting an armed conflict between the United States and Japan. . . . It should be our objective to have Japan's predatory march halted. Our course of action should, therefore, be a course in opposition to that march. That march will be halted only by the power of resistance of material obstacles and material pressures. Any nation which definitely opposes that march should be prepared in last analysis to use, if it prove necessary, armed force. . . . This country, therefore, in formulating its course of action should make it its business to be prepared if necessary to use armed force.

The American Government has during recent years been opposing Japan by use of words (appeal to principles, to rules of law, to provisions of treaties, etc.). Our Department of State may be able to get the better of the Japanese Foreign Office—though even that is not certain—in the field of argumentation, but victories on our part in that field will not halt the forward march of Japan's military machine. The fact is that unless the United States expects and intends to use weapons stronger than those of argument, continuance on our part along that line is almost certain to lead to the development of a situation in which this country will have either to accept a diplomatic defeat or find itself forced to resort to arms. The more we talk and the longer we refrain from resort to some substantial measures of positive (material) pressure toward preventing the Japanese from taking or destroying our rights, titles and interests in the Far East, the more likely will it be that resort by us to such measures at some future time—if and when—will be replied to by the Japanese with resort to armed force against us, which would, in turn, compel us to respond with armed force.

The most practicable course for us to follow would be that of giving assistance to the Chinese and withholding those things which are of assistance to the Japanese, toward prolonging and strengthening China's resistance and curtailing Japan's ability to continue military operations against China. If and when, however, we commit ourselves to that line of action, we should do so wholeheartedly and with determination. We should not take some one step without expecting, intending and being able to take further steps, many further steps, in the same direction. Such steps should include a combination of diplomatic, economic and potential military pressures. If this Government wishes to embark upon such a course, it should be prepared to consider seriously the taking of such steps as denunciation of the U.S.-Japan Commercial Treaty of 1911, repeal of the Neutrality Act, retaliatory tariff measures against Japan, placing embargoes upon trade and shipping between Japan and the United States, disposal of our naval resources in such a manner as to indicate to the Japanese Government and nation that we "mean business."

10. Ambassador to Japan Joseph Grew Opposes Economic Sanctions, December 1, 1939

Source: George McJimsey, ed., *Documentary History of the Franklin D. Roosevelt Presidency*, vol. 7., doc. 107.

Ambassador Grew disagreed with Hornbeck's position. He feared that sanctions would prove ineffective, anger Tokyo, and lead to further Japanese expansion rather than an end to it. Rather than the road of confrontation, the ambassador encouraged Washington to seek new negotiations with Tokyo to find a means to accommodate America's interests to the new realities in East Asia.

The United States is solemnly (to use that somewhat overworked Wilsonian term) committed to uphold the principles of the Nine Power

Treaty, primarily to uphold the territorial and administrative integrity of China and the Open Door. . . .

On the other side of the picture, nothing in international affairs can be more mathematically certain (if anything in international affairs is ever certain) than that Japan is not going to respect the territorial and administrative integrity of China, now or in future, has not the slightest intention of doing so and could be brought to do so only by complete defeat. Observance in practice of the Open Door is and will continue to be a matter of degree governed by expediency, not by principle. . . .

Given the situation now existing in Europe, *there does not now appear on the horizon* the possibility of such a defeat being inflicted by any nation or by any set of circumstances, military, social, economic or financial. There may be temporary setbacks or a stalemate in the military field . . . but an overwhelming debacle there is little present outlook. . . .

It is our opinion, however, that even if worse came to worst there is realization that Japan has irrevocably committed herself to the continental adventure and is determined to see it through. The majority opinion in the Embassy, which I myself share, does not believe that an American embargo, even if it covered all American exportation and importation to and from Japan, would bring about such a debacle as would cause the Japanese to relinquish their program in China. . . .

Japan is a nation of hardy warriors still inculcated with the samurai do-or-die spirit which has by tradition and inheritance become ingrained in the race. The Japanese throughout their history have faced periodic cataclysms brought about by nature and by man: earthquakes, hurricanes, floods, epidemics, the blighting of crops, and almost constant wars within and without the country. By long experience they are inured to hardships and they are inured to regimentation. Every former difficulty has been overcome. . . .

During the months since my return from the United States I have carefully and thoroughly studied opinion in Japan . . . and on one issue that opinion can definitely be said to be unanimous: the so-called "new order in East Asia" has come to stay. That term is open to wide interpretation, but the minimum conception of the term envisages permanent Japanese control of Machuria, Inner Mongolia, and North China. In the army and among certain elements of the Government and the public the conception is very much broader; those elements would exert Japanese control throughout all of China, or as much of China as can now or in future be grasped and held, including the treaty ports and the international settlements and concessions. Control in Manchuria is already crystallized through the puppet state of "Manchukuo." . . .

To await the hoped-for discrediting in Japan of the Japanese army and the Japanese military system is to await the millenium [*sic*]. . . .

So here we find ourselves squarely faced with a problem which, from all present indications, is to be permanently with us. . . . What are we going to do about it? . . .

One course envisages complete intransigence. Unless and until Japan reorientates her policy and actions, both as regards her commitments under the Nine Power Treaty . . . and her respect of American rights and interests in China, we would refuse to negotiate a new treaty of commerce and navigation and would, if public demand in the United States calls for it, impose an embargo next winter.

This course would set Japanese-American relations moving on a downward slope to a point from which it would be difficult to bring them back to normal for a long time to come; a treatyless situation, with its attending handicaps to Japanese trade, would start the movement; the imposition of an embargo would greatly accelerate it.

The other course, after endeavoring to consider the situation and outlook from all angles, I believe is in our own interests now and, so far as we can foresee the future, the wiser one to follow. We would say to Japan: "The United States concedes no right and recognizes no compromise with respect to the provisions and principles of the Nine Power Treaty. We, however, desire so far as feasible to maintain good relations with Japan. We await progressive implementation of your assurances that American rights and interests in China will be respected, not only in negative ways, such as cessation of the bombings of American property, indignities to American citizens and the more flagrant interferences with American business and trade, but also in positive ways through the presentation progressively of concrete evidence that American commercial, cultural and other rights and interests are not to be crowded out of China by Japanese measures as hitherto has appeared patently to be intentional. As soon as some definite start is made in presenting concrete evidence to the foregoing effect, we, for our part, with a view to facilitating the efforts of the Government in Tokyo to further such a program, will enter into negotiations for a new treaty of commerce and navigation and concurrently for a *modus vivendi* of limited duration to tide over a treatyless situation, *it being clearly understood that the ratification of such a treaty will depend upon future developments*, namely, the progressive implementation of such a program. . . ."

Within the next two months we are coming to a crisis in Japanese-American relations, to a possible parting of the ways. One way points straight down hill. A treatyless situation plus an embargo would exasperate the Japanese to a point where anything could happen, even serious incidents which could inflame the American people beyond endurance and which might call for war. The Japanese are so constituted and are just now in such a mood and temper that sanctions, far from intimidating, would almost certainly bring retaliation which, in turn, would lead to counter-retaliation. . . .

It is axiomatic to say that good relations between the United States and Japan are in our own interests. No purely altruistic motives are involved. In our own interests, particularly our commercial and cultural interests, we should approach this problem from a realistic and constructive standpoint. Not only on Japan's future action but on our own future action too will depend the question whether our relations with Japan are susceptible of improvement or whether they are to go straight down hill. There is no use whatever in quibbling about this, no use in refusing to face facts. The bombings of our property, the personal indignities and interferences, and some of the more flagrant violations of our commercial rights can be stemmed, but unless we are prepared to fight for it, the Open Door, as we conceive it, is not going to be kept open. We have the choice of losing everything or of saving something from the wreckage, while opening the way to a potential building up of our relations with Japan. Whatever course we elect to take should be adopted only after reaching a perfectly clear perception of where the alternative courses will lead, and then of most carefully weighing the pros and cons between them.

In brief, to sum up, I believe that we should now offer the Japanese a *modus vivendi* . . . that we should commence negotiations for a new treaty . . . [and] the Administration should withhold the laying down of an embargo against Japan unless and until it becomes evident that the efforts of the Japanese Government effectively to ameliorate the present position of American interests in China are futile and hopeless. . . .

The argument is often advanced that Japan should and can be brought to terms through isolation. The corollary is furthermore advanced that unless isolated . . . it is only a question of time before Japan continues her continental and overseas expansion, involving the Philippines, the Netherlands East Indies and other western possessions in the Far East; that the time to restrain her expansion is now.

With regard to this thesis . . . the resort to methods calculated to bring about the isolation of delinquent nations must presuppose in the final analysis the use of force.

The Conflict in Europe

11. The 1935 Neutrality Act

Source: *U.S. Statutes at Large* 49 (1935–1936): 1081–85.

Responding to the growing fears of war in Europe, Congress passed a Neutrality Act designed to prevent the United States from being drawn into another European war by curtailing the type of interactions American businesses and individuals could have with nations at war.

Resolved by the Senate and House of Representatives of the United States of America in Congress assembled, That upon the outbreak or during the progress of war between, or among, two or more foreign states, the President shall proclaim such fact, and it shall thereafter be unlawful to export arms, ammunition, or implements of war from any place in the United States, or possessions of the United States, to any port of such belligerent states, or to any neutral port for transshipment to, or for the use of, a belligerent country. . . .

Sec. 3. Whenever the President shall issue the proclamation provided for in section 1 of this Act, thereafter it shall be unlawful for any American vessel to carry any arms, ammunition, or implementation of war to any port or the belligerent countries named in such proclamation as being at war, or to any neutral port for transshipment to, or for the use of, a belligerent country. . . .

Sec. 6. Whenever, during any war in which the United States is neutral, the President shall find that the maintenance of peace between the United States and foreign nations, or the protection of the lives of citizens of the United States, or the protection of the commercial interests of the United States and its citizens, or the security of the United States requires that the American citizens should refrain from traveling as passengers on the vessels of any belligerent nation, he shall so proclaim, and thereafter no citizen of the United States shall travel on any vessel of any belligerent nation except at his own risk, unless in accordance with such rules and regulations as the President shall prescribe. . . .

12. President Roosevelt's December 17, 1940, Press Conference

Source: Rosenman, *Public Papers and Addresses of Franklin D. Roosevelt*, vol. 9, 604–8.

In his December 17 press conference, President Roosevelt set out the concept behind the lend-lease policy. Roosevelt saw the policy as a way to get desperately needed aid to Great Britain while also avoiding the problems of loans that fueled neutralist opposition and had led to many of the global economic problems after World War I.

Now, what I am trying to do is to eliminate the dollar sign, and that is something brand new in the thoughts of practically everybody in the room, I think—get rid of the silly, foolish old dollar sign. All right!

Well, let me give you an illustration: Suppose my neighbor's home catches fire, and I have got a length of garden hose four or five hundred feet away; but, my Heaven, if he can take my garden hose and connect it up with his hydrant, I may help him put out his fire. Now what do I do? I don't say to him before the operation, "Neighbor, my garden hose cost me $15; you have got to pay me $15 for it." What is the transaction that goes on? I don't want $15—I want my garden hose back after the fire is over. All right. If it goes through the fire all right, intact, without any damage to it, he gives it back to me and thanks me very much for the use of it. But suppose it gets smashed up—holes in it—during the fire; we don't have to have too much formality about it, but I say to him, "I was glad to lend you that hose; I see I can't use it any more, it's all smashed up." He says, "How many feet of it were there?" I tell him, "there were 150 feet of it." He said, "All right, I will replace it." Now, it I get a nice garden hose back, I am in pretty good shape. In other words, if you lend certain munitions and get the munitions back at the end of the war, if they are intact—haven't been hurt—you are all right; if they have been damaged or deteriorated or lost completely, it seems to me you come out pretty well if you have them replaced by the fellow that you have lent them to. . . .

13. President Roosevelt's "Arsenal of Democracy" Address, December 29, 1940

Source: McJimsey, *Documentary History of the Franklin D. Roosevelt Presidency*, vol. 2, *The Lend-Lease Act, December 1940–April 1941*, doc. 10.

Speaking to the nation for the first time since the election, Roosevelt set out his under-standing of the nation's "national security" needs and how lend-lease fit into his concept of national defense. Arguing that any defeat of Great Britain would immediately imperil the nation, the president called upon the United States to become the "arsenal of democracy."

This is not a fireside chat on war. It is a talk on national security; because the nub of the whole purpose of your President is to keep you now, and your children later, and your grandchildren much later, out of a last-ditch war for the preservation of American independence and all of the things that American independence means to you and to me and to ours. . . .

Never before since Jamestown and Plymouth Rock has our American civilization been in such danger as now.

For, on September 27, 1940, by an agreement signed in Berlin, three powerful nations, two in Europe and one in Asia, joined themselves together in the threat that if the United States interfered with or blocked the expansion program of these three nations—a program aimed at world control—they would unite in ultimate action against the United States.

The Nazi masters of Germany have made it clear that they intend not only to dominate all life and thought in their own country, but also to enslave the whole of Europe, and then to use the resources of Europe to dominate the rest of the world. . . .

In other words, the Axis not merely admits but proclaims that there can be no ultimate peace between their philosophy of government and our philosophy of government. . . .

Some of our people like to believe that wars in Europe and in Asia are of no concern to us. But it is a matter of most vital concern to us that European and Asiatic war-makers should not gain control of the oceans which lead to this hemisphere. . . .

If Great Britain goes down, the Axis Powers will control the continents of Europe, Asia, Africa, Australasia, and the high seas—and they will be in a position to bring enormous military and naval resources against this hemisphere. It is no exaggeration to say that all of us in the Americas would be living at the point of a gun—a gun loaded with explosive bullets, economic as well as military.

We should enter upon a new and terrible era in which the whole world, our hemisphere included, would be run by threats of brute force. To survive in such a world, we would have to convert ourselves permanently into a militaristic power on the basis of war economy.

Some of us like to believe that even if Great Britain falls, we are still safe, because of the broad expanse of the Atlantic and the Pacific.

But the width of these oceans is not what it was in the days of clipper ships. At one point between Africa and Brazil the distance is less than from Washington to Denver—five hours for the latest type of bomber. And at the North of the Pacific Ocean, America and Asia almost touch each other. . . .

There are those who say that the Axis powers would never have any desire to attack the Western Hemisphere. This is the same dangerous form of wishful thinking which has destroyed the powers of resistance of so many conquered peoples. . . .

The experience of the past two years has proven beyond doubt that no nation can appease the Nazis. No man can tame a tiger into a kitten by stroking it. There can be no appeasement with ruthlessness. There can be no reasoning with an incendiary bomb. We know now that a nation can have peace with the Nazis only at the price of total surrender. . . .

The American appeasers ignore the warning to be found in the fate of Austria, Czechoslovakia, Poland, Norway, Belgium, the Netherlands, Denmark, and France. They tell you that the Axis powers are going to win anyway; that all this bloodshed in the world could be saved; and that the United States might just as well throw its influence into the scale of a dictated peace, and get the best out of it that we can.

They call it a "negotiated peace." Nonsense! Is it a negotiated peace if a gang of outlaws surrounds your community and on threat of extermination makes you pay tribute to save your own skins? . . .

Thinking in terms of today and tomorrow, I make the direct statement to the American people that there is far less chance of the United States getting into war if we do all we can now to support the nations defending themselves against attack by the Axis than if we acquiesce in their defeat, submit tamely to an Axis victory, and wait our turn to be the object of attack in another war later on.

If we are completely honest with ourselves, we must admit there is risk in *any* course we may take. But I deeply believe that the great majority of our people agree that the course that I advocate involves the least risk now and the greatest hope for world peace in the future. . . .

Democracy's fight against world conquest is being greatly aided, and must be more greatly aided, by the rearmament of the United States and by sending every ounce and every ton of munitions and supplies that we can possibly spare to help the defenders who are on the front lines. . . .

We are planning our own defense with the utmost urgency; and in its vast scale we must integrate the war needs of Britain and the other free nations resisting aggression. . . .

As planes and ships and guns and shells are produced, your government, with its defense experts, can then determine how best to use them to defend this hemisphere. The decision as to how much shall be sent abroad and how much shall remain at home must be made on the basis of our over-all military necessities.

We must be the great arsenal of democracy. For us this is an emergency as serious as war itself. We must apply ourselves to our task with the same resolution, the same sense of urgency, the same spirit of patriotism and sacrifice as we would show were we at war. . . .

14. President Roosevelt Sets Out the Four Freedoms, January 6, 1941

Source: McJimsey, *Documentary History of the Franklin D. Roosevelt Presidency,* vol. 2, doc. 11.

In his State of the Union message, Roosevelt outlined the threat to the United States and the values that the nation was defending, what he termed the "four freedoms."

I address you, the Members of the Seventy-Seventh Congress, at a moment unprecedented in the history of the Union. I use the word "unprecedented," because at no previous time has American security been as seriously threatened from without as it is today. . . .

Every realist knows that the democratic way of life is at this moment being directly assailed in every part of the world—assailed either by arms or by secret spreading of poisonous ideas by those whose true purpose is to destroy unity and promote discord in nations still at peace. . . .

I have recently pointed out how quickly the tempo of modern warfare could bring into our very midst the physical attack, which we must expect if the dictator nations win this war. This country and all the people of this Hemisphere know by now how direct a threat against us lies in the formal tri-partite alliance of the aggressor nations of the world. . . .

Let us say to the democracies: America stands behind you. America is putting forth her energies, her resources and her organizing powers to give you the strength to regain and maintain a free world. America will send you, in ever increasing numbers, ships, planes, tanks and guns, food and medical supplies. . . .

In the future days which we seek to make secure, we look forward to a world founded fundamentally upon four essential human freedoms.

The first is freedom of speech and expression everywhere in the world.

The second is freedom of every person to worship God in his own way everywhere in the world.

The third is freedom from want—which translated into world terms means economic understandings which will secure to every nation a healthy peace time life for its inhabitants—everywhere in the world.

The fourth is freedom from fear—which translated into world terms means a world-wide reduction of armaments to such a point and in such a thorough fashion that no nation will be in a position to commit an act of physical aggression against any neighbor—anywhere in the world. . . .

15. Congressional Opponents of Lend-Lease

Source: U.S. Senate, *Congressional Record* 87, pt. 1, 1109–10; U.S. Senate, *Congressional Record* 87, pt. 2, 1281–82.

President Roosevelt's lend-lease proposal led to the final debate between internationalists and proponents of neutrality. Opponents argued that lend-lease was a detriment to the national defense as it would give away valuable American supplies, would be wasted as a German victory was assured, and would bring the United States into the war in Europe. Moreover, they feared an expansion of executive power at the expense of congressional oversight. The excerpts below from the debates on February 18 and February 22 in the Senate set out some of the central concerns of the opposition to the lend-lease bill.

Senator Nye: As I listened to the speech in which the Senator from Kentucky [Mr. Barkley] presented this bill for passage I heard him plead . . . that we should "grant a few necessary powers" conferred upon the President in order to attain the ends which this bill seeks. Incidentally, Mr. President, I could not but remark that, while the bill itself states that its purpose is "to promote the defense of the United States, and for other purposes," the interest of the Senator from Kentucky was apparently centered on those "other purposes"—by which I take it he would mean "licking the daylights" out of Adolf Hitler—because he said almost nothing in his speech about "the defense of the United States." But I do not care very much about that; I have grown accustomed to hearing men who favor further steps toward war say one thing when they really mean another, and when a Senator such as the Senator from Kentucky really means that what he cares most about is seeing Hitler "licked," I am glad to have him come right out and say so. It clears the atmosphere; it helps us to know where we are and what we are really dealing with in this debate. It would help still more, Mr. President, if we could now have this bill itself honestly labeled, and call it a bill to put the United States fully into the bloody business of licking Adolf Hitler. . . .

Here is the crux of this whole debate. Is it true that all this bill would do would be to confer on the Executive a few, only a few, and those necessary powers—powers which Congress, having once given away, would never miss, and whose passing from the control of the legislative to the control of the executive branch of the Government would cause no significant change whatever in our constitutional form of government? Is that true?

Of course it is not true. Such a claim, that only "a few necessary powers" are involved, is an attempted hoax on this body and on the American people—as gigantic and terrible a hoax as the claim that this is a bill to defend the United States. . . .

First. To begin with, note that the bill will, if enacted, give the President power to make military alliances with any nations anywhere in the world. Yes; by himself, without any check from this body or any other source, he alone may arrange military alliances with any governments or groups of governments on earth. . . .

Second. Under the bill the President would have power to give away outright . . . the United States navy—not only destroyers, but every warship we possess. . .

Third. The power to dispose of every scrap of defense material of the Army.

Fourth. The power to part with every airplane in our air service. . . .

Senator Clark: The public has been led to believe that this bill simply provides for "aid to Britain" by "means short of war". . . .

Much as I admire the heroism of the British defense of their own islands . . . I am entirely unwilling to commit this country to a defense of the

British Empire around the world. I am utterly unwilling to turn over to them articles which we might vitally need for our own defense. . . . I protest that our taxpayers should not be called upon to assume the burden of paying for the defense of the British Empire when the financial resources of the Empire have not been exhausted and when they have other assets, in the shape of possessions in this hemisphere not very valuable to them but which might be priceless to us which they could turn over to us.

Senator Taft: Above all, the bill puts the President in a position where he can run the war. . . . The proponents of the bill have refused to limit his discretion as to the nation which may be aided. He will have power to plunge into war millions of people now at peace. He can make himself the great protagonist of the forces opposing Hitler. . . .

Secretary Knox and Secretary Stimson assert that the defeat of Britain would mean an immediate attack by Germany on the United States, likely to be successful. I utterly disagree with them, but if that is their belief, the only logical course is for us to enter the war now. The truth is these gentlemen have always been for war. . . . Secretary Stimson advocated convoys and the use of American bases by the British fleet, in June 1940. . . .

The attacks on appeasers are an attempt to suppress and strangle the voices of those opposed to war. There is here no question of appeasement. Appeasement means the yielding to demands with the hope that such yielding will prevent further aggression. Germany has made no demands on the United States; has made no attack on the United States. We are considering the question whether we shall go to war with a country which has taken no hostile step in the direction of the United States and whose violent language has only matched our own. The American appeasers are those who are vainly striving to satisfy Britain with money and materials in the hope that they may avoid the sending of men.

16. The Atlantic Charter

Source: Rosenman, *Public Papers and Addresses of Franklin D. Roosevelt*, vol. 10, 310–14.

On August 14, the White House released the text of the Atlantic Charter, agreed to by President Roosevelt and British prime minister Winston Churchill during their recent meeting off the Canadian coast. The Atlantic Charter set out the liberal, internationalist war aims of the Western allies.

The President of the United States of America and the Prime Minister, Mr. Churchill, representing His Majesty's Government in the United Kingdom, being met together, deem it right to make known certain common principles in the national policies of their respective countries on which they base their hopes for a better future for the world.

First, their countries seek no aggrandizement, territorial or other;

Second, they desire to see no territorial changes that do not accord with the freely expressed wishes of the peoples concerned;

Third, they respect the right of all peoples to choose the form of government under which they will live; and they wish to see sovereign rights and self government restored to those who have been forcibly denied of them;

Fourth, they will endeavor, with due respect for their existing obligations, to further the enjoyment by all States, great or small, victor or vanquished, of access, on equal terms, to the trade and to the raw materials of the world which are needed for their economic prosperity;

Fifth, they desire to bring about the fullest collaboration between all nations in the economic field with the object of securing, for all, improved labor standards, economic advancement and social security;

Sixth, after the final destruction of the Nazi tyranny, they hope to see established a peace which will afford to all nations the means of dwelling in safety within their own boundaries, and which will afford assurance that all the men in all the lands may live out their lives in freedom from fear and want;

Seventh, such a peace should enable all men to transverse the high seas and oceans without hindrance;

Eighth, they believe that all of the nations of the world, for realistic as well as spiritual reasons must come to the abandonment of the use of force. Since no future peace can be maintained if land, sea or air armaments continue to be employed by nations which threaten, or may threaten, aggression outside of their frontiers, they believe, pending the establishment of a wider and permanent system of general security, that the disarmament of such nations is essential. They will likewise aid and encourage all other practicable measures which will lighten for peace-loving peoples the crushing burden of armaments.

The Coming of War With Japan

17. Exchange of Letters Between Ambassador Grew and President Roosevelt on Japan's Threat to the United States

Source: President's Secretary File: Country File, Japan, Box 9, FDRL.

On December 14, 1940, Ambassador Grew wrote the president appraising the prospects of pressure on Japan and asking for Roosevelt's thoughts on the growing tensions between Washington and Tokyo. President Roosevelt replied on January 21, 1941, setting his policy toward Japan into the larger context of a world at war.

Grew to Roosevelt:

After eight years of effort to build up something permanently constructive in American-Japanese relations, I find that diplomacy has been defeated by trends and forces utterly beyond its control. . . . Japan has become openly and unashamedly one of the predatory nations and part of a system which aims to wreck about everything that the United States stands for. Only insuperable obstacles will not prevent the Japanese from digging in permanently in China and from pushing the southward advance. . . . Economic obstacles, such as may arise from American embargoes, will seriously handicap Japan in the long run, but meanwhile they tend to push the Japanese onward in the forlorn hope of making themselves economically self-sufficient. . . .

It therefore appears that sooner or later, unless we are prepared . . . to withdraw bag and baggage from the entire sphere of "Greater East Asia including the South Seas" (which God forbid), we are bound eventually to come to a head-on clash with Japan.

A progressively firm policy on our part will entail inevitable risks . . . but in my opinion those risks are less in degree than the far greater future dangers which we would face if we were to follow a policy of laisser-faire. . . .

The principal point at issue, as I see it, is not whether we must call a halt to the Japanese program, but when.

It is important constantly to bear in mind the fact that if we take measures "short of war" with no real intention to carry those measures to their final conclusion if necessary, such lack of intention will be all too obvious to the Japanese who will proceed undeterred, and even with greater incentive, on their way. Only if they become certain that we mean to fight if called upon to do so will our preliminary measures stand some chance of proving effective and of removing the necessity of force. . . .

Roosevelt to Grew:

The fundamental proposition is that we must recognize that the hostilities in Europe, in Africa, and in Asia are all parts of a single world conflict. We must, consequently, recognize that our interests are menaced both in Europe and in the Far East. We are engaged in the task of defending our way of life and our vital national interests wherever they are seriously endangered. Our strategy of self-defense must be a global strategy which takes account of every front and takes advantage of every opportunity to contribute to our total security.

You suggest as one of the chief factors in the problem of our attitude toward Japan the question of whether our getting into war with Japan would so handicap our help to Britain in Europe as to make the difference to Britain between victory and defeat. In this connection it seems to me that we must consider whether, if Japan should gain possession of the region of the Netherlands East Indies and the Malay Peninsula, the chances of England winning in her struggle with Germany would not be decreased thereby. . . . The British need assistance along the lines of our generally established policies at many points, assistance which in the case of the Far East is certainly well within the realm of "possibility" so far as the capacity of the United States is concerned. Their defense strategy must in the nature of things be global. Our strategy of giving them assistance toward ensuring our own security must envisage both sending of supplies to England and helping to prevent a closing of channels of communication to and from various parts of the world, so that other important sources of supply will not be denied to the British and be added to the assets of the other side. . . .

The problems which we face are so vast and so interrelated that any attempt even to state them compels one to think in terms of five continents and seven seas. In conclusion, I must emphasize that, our problem being one of defense, we can not lay down hard and fast plans. As each new development occurs we must, in the light of the circumstances then existing, decide when and where and how we can most effectively marshal and make use of our resources.

18. Japanese Imperial Conference, July 2, 1941

Source: U.S. Congress, *Hearings Before the Joint Committee on the Investigation of the Pearl Harbor Attack*, 79th Cong., 1st and 2nd sess. (Washington: Government Printing Office, 1946), pt. 20, 4018–19.

The following document is a summary of the decisions made at a meeting of Japanese government and military officials contemplating war with Great Britain and the United States. It led to the taking of the rest of Indochina later that month.

I. Policy
1. The Imperial Government is determined to follow a policy which will result in the establishment of the Greater East Asia Co-Prosperity Sphere and world peace, no matter what international developments take place.
2. The Imperial Government will continue its efforts to effect a settlement of the China Incident and seek to establish a solid basis for the security and preservation of the nation. This will involve an advance into the Southern Regions [Southeast Asia]. . . .
3. The Imperial Government will carry out the above program no matter what obstacles may be encountered.

II. Summary
1. Steps will be taken to bring pressure on the Chiang Regime from the Southern approaches in order to bring about its surrender. . . .
2. In order to guarantee national security and preservation, the Imperial Government will continue all necessary diplomatic negotiations with reference to the southern regions and also carry out various other plans as may be necessary. In case the diplomatic negotiations break down, preparations for a war with England and America will also be carried forward. . . .
3. Our attitude with reference to the German-Soviet War will be based on the spirit of the Tri-Partite Pact. However, we will not enter the conflict for some time but will steadily proceed with military preparations against the Soviets and decide our final attitude independently. . . .
4. In carrying out the preceding article all plans, especially the use of armed forces, will be carried out in such a way as to place no serious obstacles in the path of our basic military preparations for a war with England and America. . . .

19. Japanese Leaders Discuss Secretary of State Hull's Comments to Japan's Ambassador

Source: Nobutaka Ike, ed. and trans., *Japan's Decision for War* (Stanford, CA: Stanford University Press, 1967), 94–102.

On June 21, Hull met with Japan's Ambassador Nomura Kichisaburô to discuss Tokyo's alliance with Berlin and relations between the United States and Japan. The American secretary of state bluntly criticized Japan's policy as aggression, stated that Japan needed to change its cabinet, and noted that the United States would only negotiate if Japan came up with a new policy that sought cooperation and peaceful relations in East Asia. The Japanese leaders discussed Hull's comments on July 10 and 12.

Advisor to the Foreign Minister Saito Yoshie: The present world, divided into those who are for the maintenance of the status quo and those who are for its destruction, the democracies and the totalitarian states, is in the midst of a war. Hull's reply is for the status quo and for democracy. It is obvious that America sent it after consultation with Britain and China. Thus I think the countries that are for the status quo are getting together to put pressure on Japan. On the matter of Sino-Japanese negotiations, the United States hopes to make us negotiate on the basis of conditions existing prior to the China Incident. . . .

The Americans think that Manchuria should revert to China. This proposal says, in effect, that Japan and China should negotiate after Japan has renounced the joint declaration made by Japan, Manchukuo, and China. . . .

Foreign Minister Matsuoka: Hull's "Statement" is outrageous. . . . Acceptance of the American proposal would threaten the establishment of a Greater East Asian Co-prosperity Sphere, and this would be a very grave matter. . . .

I believe that the American attitude will not change, no matter what attitude Japan takes. It is the nature of the American people to take advantage of you if you show weakness. Therefore, I believe it is better to take a strong position on this occasion. . . .

War Minister Hideki Tojo: Even if there is no hope, I would like to persist to the very end. It know it is difficult; but it will be intolerable if we cannot establish the Greater East Asian Co-prosperity Sphere and settle the

China Incident. Because of the Tri-Partite Pact, can't we at least prevent the formal participation of the United States in the war? . . . If we sincerely convey to the Americans what we, as Japanese, believe to be right, won't they be inwardly moved? . . .

Navy Minister Koshiro Oikawa: According to Navy reports, it appears that Secretary of State Hull and others are not prepared to provoke a Pacific war. Since Japan does not wish to engage in a Pacific war, isn't there room for negotiations?

20. Japan's Decision to Take French Indochina

Source: U.S. Congress, *Hearings Before the Joint Committee on the Investigation of the Pearl Harbor Attack*, pt. 12: 9.

In a July 31, 1941, cable to the Japanese embassy in Washington, D.C., Tokyo argued that mounting pressures against Japan made it necessary for it to seize French Indochina.

Commercial and economic relations between Japan and third countries, led by England and the United States, are gradually becoming so horribly strained that we cannot endure it much longer. Consequently, our Empire, to save its very life, must take measures to secure the raw materials of the South Seas. Our Empire must immediately take steps to break asunder this ever-strengthening chair of encirclement which is being woven under the guidance and with the participation of England and the United States. . . . This is why we decided to obtain military bases in French Indo-China and to have our troops occupy that territory.

21. Roosevelt Warns Japan to Cease Its Expansion

Source: *FRUS: Japan, 1931–1941*, vol. 2, 556–57.

In response to Japan's taking of Indochina, on August 17, 1941, President Roosevelt warned Ambassador Nomura that the United States would not tolerate any further expansion by Japan.

The Government of Japan has continued its military activities and its disposals of armed forces at various points in the Far East and has occupied Indochina with its military, air and naval forces. . . .

Such being the case, this Government now finds it necessary to say to the Government of Japan that if the Japanese Government takes any further steps in pursuance of a policy or program of military domination by force or threat of force of neighboring countries, the Government of the United States will be compelled to take immediately any and all steps which it may deem necessary toward safeguarding the legitimate rights and interests of the United States and American nationals toward insuring the safety and security of the United States.

22. Japan Prepares for War

Source: U.S. Congress, *Hearings Before the Joint Committee on the Investigation of the Pearl Harbor Attack*, pt. 20: 4022.

On September 6, 1941, in accordance with the decisions reached on July 2, the Japanese Imperial Conference began final preparations for war while continuing negotiations with the United States.

In view of the increasingly critical situation, especially the aggressive plans being carried out by America, England, Holland and other countries, the situation in Soviet Russia and the Empire's latent potentialities, the Japanese Government will proceed as follows in carrying out its plans for the southern territories.

1. Determined not to be deterred by the possibility of being involved in a war with America (and England and Holland) in order to secure our national existence, we will proceed with war preparations so that they [will] be completed approximately toward the end of October.

2. At the same time, we will endeavor by every possible diplomatic means to have our demands agreed to by America and England. . . .

3. If by the early part of October there is no reasonable hope of having our demands agreed to in the diplomatic negotiations mentioned above, we will immediately make up our minds to get ready for war against America (and England and Holland).

I. Japan's Minimum Demands in her Negotiations with America (and England).

1. American and England shall not intervene in or obstruct a settlement by Japan of the China incident. . . .

3. America and England will cooperate with Japan in her attempt to obtain needed raw materials. . . .

23. Japan's Final Negotiating Terms

Source: *FRUS: Japan, 1931–1941*, vol. 2, 755–56.

Ambassador Nomura met with Secretary of State Hull on November 20, 1941, to deliver Tokyo's final negotiation position. As the next document shows, this effort was rejected by the United States.

1.   Both the Governments of Japan and the United States undertake not to make any armed advancement into any of the regions in the South-eastern Asia and the Southern Pacific area excepting the part of French Indo-China where the Japanese troops are stationed at present.

2.   The Japanese Government undertakes to withdraw its troops now stationed in French Indo-China upon either the restoration of peace between Japan and China or the establishment of an equitable peace in the Pacific area.

     In the meantime the Government of Japan declares that it is prepared to remove its troops now stationed in the southern part of French Indo-China to the northern part of the said territory upon the conclusion of the present arrangement. . . .

3.   The Governments of Japan and the United States shall cooperate with a view to securing the acquisition of those goods and commodities which the two countries need in Netherlands East Indies.

4.   The Government of Japan and the United States mutually undertake to restore their commercial relations to those prevailing prior to the freezing of the assets.

     The Government of the United States shall supply Japan a required quantity of oil.

5.   The Government of the United States undertakes to refrain from such measures and actions as will be prejudicial to the endeavors for the restoration of general peace between Japan and China.

24. The United States Rejects Japan's Final Offer

Source: *FRUS: Japan, 1931–1941*, vol. 2, 768–72.

President Roosevelt and Secretary of State Hull met with Japanese Ambassador Nomura and Kurusu Sabura on November 27, 1941, to present the U.S. response to Japan's final offer. While Roosevelt expressed his appreciation for the efforts of the "peace element" in Japan, he laid the blame for the crisis on Japan's policy of aggression and the militarist groups in Tokyo. Roosevelt's and Hull's comments make up the first document below. The second document is the formal American policy proposal to Japan for the continuation of negotiations. Given the demands made, most notably for a Japanese withdrawal from China, Roosevelt and Hull knew this would be rejected and that war was now inevitable.

The President proceeded to express the grateful appreciation of himself and of this Government to the peace element in Japan which has worked hard in support of the movement to establish a peaceful settlement in the Pacific area. . . . The President added that in the United States most people want a peaceful solution of all matters in the Pacific area. He said that he does not give up yet although the situation is serious and that fact should be recognized. He then referred to the conversations since April which have been carried on here with the Japanese Ambassador in an attempt to deal with the difficulties. The President added that some of these difficulties at times have the effect of a cold bath on the United States Government and people, such as the recent occupation of Indochina by the Japanese and recent movements and utterances of the Japanese slanting wholly in the direction of conquest by force and ignoring the whole question of a peaceful settlement and the principles underlying it. . . .

We remain convinced that Japan's own best interests will not be served by following Hitlerism and courses of aggression. . . . If, however, Japan should unfortunately decide to follow Hitlerism and courses of aggression, we are convinced beyond any shadow of doubt that Japan will be the ultimate loser. . . .

[Hull] made it clear that . . . everyone knows that the Japanese slogans of co-prosperity, new order in East Asia and a controlling influence in certain areas, are all terms to express in a camouflaged manner the policy of force and conquest by Japan and the domination by military agencies of the political, economic, social and moral affairs of each of the populations conquered; and that as long as they move in that direction . . . there could not be any real progress on a peaceful course.

Section I

Draft Mutual Declaration of Policy

The Government of the United States and the Government of Japan both being solicitous for the peace of the Pacific affirm that their national policies are directed toward lasting and extensive peace throughout the Pacific area, that they have no territorial designs in that area, that they have no intention of threatening other countries or of using military force aggressively against any neighboring nation, and that, accordingly, in their national policies they will actively support and give practical application to the following fundamental principles upon which their relations with each other and with all other governments are based:

1. The principle of inviolability of territorial integrity and sovereignty of each and all nations.

2. The principle of non-interference in the internal affairs of other countries.

3. The principle of equality, including equality of commercial opportunity and treatment.

4. The principle of reliance upon international cooperation and conciliation for the prevention and pacific settlement of controversies and for improvement of international conditions by peaceful methods and processes. . . .

Section II

Steps to be Taken by the Government of the United States and the Government of Japan.

The Government of the United States and the Government of Japan propose to take steps as follows:

1. The Government of the United States and the Government of Japan will endeavor to conclude a multilateral non-aggression pact among the British Empire, China, Japan, the Netherlands, the Soviet Union, Thailand, and the United States.

2. Both Governments will endeavor to conclude among the American, British, Chinese, Japanese, the Netherland and Thai Governments an agreement whereunder each of the Governments would pledge itself to respect the territorial integrity of French Indochina. . . .

3. The Government of Japan will withdraw its military, naval, air and police forces from China and from Indochina.

4.   The Government of the United States and the Government of Japan will not support—militarily, politically, economically—any government or regime in China other than the National Government of the Republic of China with capital temporarily at Chungking.

5.   Both Governments will give up all extraterritorial rights in China. . . .

6.   The Government of the United States and the Government of Japan will enter into negotiation for the conclusion between the United States and Japan of a trade agreement, based upon reciprocal most-favored-nation treatment and reduction of trade barriers by both countries. . . .

7.   The Government of the United States and the Government of Japan will, respectively, remove the freezing restrictions on Japanese funds in the United States and on American funds in Japan. . . .

9.   Both Governments will agree that no agreement which either has concluded with any third power or powers shall be interpreted by it in such a way as to conflict with the fundamental purpose of this agreement, the establishment and preservation of peace throughout the Pacific area. . . .

25. President Roosevelt's War Message, December 8, 1941

Source: *Personal Papers and Addresses of Franklin D. Roosevelt, 1941, 514–515. The day after Pearl Harbor, President Roosevelt asked Congress for a declaration of war against Japan. His war message firmly placed the blame for hostilities upon Japan and promised victory in the fighting to come.*

Yesterday, December 7, 1941—a date which will live in infamy—the United States of America was suddenly and deliberately attacked by naval and air forces of the Empire of Japan.

The United States was at peace with that Nation and, at the solicitation of Japan, was still in conversation with its Government and its Emperor looking toward the maintenance of peace in the Pacific. . . .

It will be recorded that the distance to Hawaii from Japan makes it obvious that the attack was deliberately planned many days or even weeks ago. During the intervening time the Japanese Government has deliberately sought to deceive the United States by false statements and expressions of hope for continued peace.

The attack yesterday on the Hawaiian Islands has caused severe damage to American naval and military forces. Very many American lives have been lost. In addition American ships have been reported torpedoed on the high seas between San Francisco and Honolulu.

Yesterday the Japanese Government also launched an attack against Malaya.

Last night Japanese forces attacked Hong Kong.

Last night Japanese forces attacked Guam.

Last night Japanese forces attacked the Philippine Islands.

Last night the Japanese attacked Wake Island.

This morning the Japanese attacked Midway Island.

Japan has, therefore, undertaken a surprise offensive extending throughout the Pacific area. The facts of yesterday speak for themselves. The people of the United States have already formed their opinions and well understand the implications to the very life and safety of our Nation.

As Commander-in-Chief of the Army and Navy I have directed that all measures be taken for our defense.

Always will we remember the character of the onslaught against us.

No matter how long it may take us to overcome this premeditated invasion, the American people in their righteous might will win through to absolute victory.

I believe I interpret the will of the Congress and of the people when I assert that we will not only defend ourselves to the uttermost but will make very certain that this form of treachery shall never endanger us again.

Hostilities exist. There is no blinking at the fact that our people, our territory, and our interests are in grave danger.

With confidence in our armed forces—with the unbounded determination of our people—we will gain the inevitable triumph—so help us God.

I ask that the Congress declare that since the unprovoked and dastardly attack by Japan on Sunday, December seventh, a state of war has existed between the United States and the Japanese Empire.

NOTES

Introduction

1. Samuel I. Rosenman, ed., *The Public Papers and Addresses of Franklin D. Roosevelt,* vol. 6, *1937: The Constitution Prevails* (New York: Random House, 1941), 406–11.

2. George McJimsey, ed., *Documentary History of the Franklin D. Roosevelt Presidency,* vol. 2, *The Lend-Lease Act, December 1940–April 1941* (Bethesda, MD: University Publications of America, 2001), 71, 89–90.

3. Excellent discussions of the shifting debates and interpretations of Roosevelt's foreign policy leading up to World War II can be found in Wayne S. Cole, "American Entry Into World War II: A Historiographical Appraisal," *Mississippi Valley Historical Review* 43 (March 1957): 595–617; Justus D. Doenecke, "Beyond Polemics: An Historiographical Re-Appraisal of American Entry Into World War II," *History Teacher* 12 (February 1979): 217–51; Gerald K. Haines, "Roads to War: United States Foreign Policy, 1931–1941," in Gerald K. Haines and Samuel Walker, eds., *American Foreign Relations: A Historiographical Review* (Westport, CT: Greenwood Press, 1981), 159–85; Ernest C. Bolt Jr., "Isolation, Expansion, and Peace: American Foreign Policy Between the Wars," in Haines and Walker, *American Foreign Relations,* 133–57; J. Garry Clifford, "Both Ends of the Telescope: New Perspectives on FDR and American Entry Into World War II," *Diplomatic History* 13 (Spring 1989): 213–30; Justus D. Doenecke, "U.S. Policy and the European War, 1939–1941," *Diplomatic History* 19 (Fall 1995): 664–98; Michael A. Barnhart, "The Origins of World War II in Asia and the Pacific: Synthesis Impossible?" *Diplomatic History* 20 (Spring 1996): 241–60; and David Reynolds, *From Munich to Pearl Harbor: Roosevelt's*

America and the Origins of the Second World War (Chicago: Ivan R. Dee, 2001), 5–11.

4.   Robert Divine, *The Reluctant Belligerent: American Entry Into World War II*, 2nd ed. (New York: Wiley, 1972); Justus D. Doenecke and John E. Wiltz, *From Isolation to War, 1931–1941*, 3rd ed. (Wheeling, IL: Harlan Davidson, 2003); Robert Dallek, *Franklin D. Roosevelt and American Foreign Policy, 1932–1945* (New York: Oxford University Press, 1979); Reynolds, *From Munich to Pearl Harbor.*

Chapter 1

1.   Daniel M. Smith, *The Great Departure: The United States and World War I, 1914–1920* (New York: Wiley, 1965).

2.   Henry L. Stimson, "The United States and the Other American Republics," February 6, 1931 (Washington, DC: Government Printing Office, 1931).

3.   Merlo J. Pusey, *Charles Evans Hughes* (New York: Macmillan, 1951), 531; Charles Evans Hughes, *Our Relations to the Nations of the Western Hemisphere* (Princeton, NJ: Princeton University Press, 1928), 4, 50.

4.   U.S. Department of State, *Foreign Relations of the United States: Japan, 1931–1941* (Washington, DC: Government Printing Office, 1943), vol. 1, 76 (hereafter *FRUS* followed by the year, volume number, and page number).

Chapter 2

1.   In Edgar B. Nixon, ed., *Franklin D. Roosevelt and Foreign Affairs*, vol. 1 (Cambridge, MA: Belknap Press of Harvard University Press, 1969), 19.

2.   Cordell Hull, *The Memoirs of Cordell Hull*, vol. 1 (New York: Macmillan, 1948), 81, 355, 365.

3.   Helmuth Carol Engelbrecht and Frank Cleary Hanighen, *Merchants of Death: A Study of the International Armament Industry* (New York: Dodd, Mead & Company, 1934); George Seldes, *Iron, Blood and Profits: An Exposure of the World-Wide Munitions Racket* (New York: Harper & Brothers, 1934).

4.   Howard Jablon, *Crossroads of Decision: The State Department and Foreign Policy, 1933–1937* (Lexington: University Press of Kentucky, 1983), 87–88.

5.   Rosenman, *Public Papers and Addresses of Franklin D. Roosevelt*, 4: 345–46.

6.   Hull, *Memoirs*, 229–30.

7.   Quoted in Robert Divine, *The Illusion of Neutrality: Franklin D. Roosevelt and the Struggle Over the Arms Embargo* (Chicago: University of Chicago Press, 1962), 115.

8.   David F. Schmitz, *The United States and Fascist Italy, 1922–1940* (Chapel Hill: University of North Carolina Press, 1988).

9. Nixon, *Franklin D. Roosevelt and Foreign Affairs*, 1: 269, 265.

10. Quoted in David M. Kennedy, *Freedom From Fear: The American People in the Depression and War, 1929–1945* (New York: Oxford University Press, 1999), 373, 123.

11. "Uncle Sam as Good Neighbor," *New Republic* 77 (1933): 240.

12. Nixon, *Franklin D. Roosevelt and Foreign Affairs*, 1: 20.

13. H. Freeman Matthews to Cordell Hull, February 26, 1934, 837.00B/118, in U.S. Department of State, Record Group 59: General Records of the Department of State, National Archives, College Park, MD.

14. Joseph Grew to Cordell Hull, May 11, 1933, and Cordell Hull to Franklin D. Roosevelt, May 27, 1933, President's Secretary File (hereafter PSF): Japan, Box 42, Franklin D. Roosevelt Presidential Library, Hyde Park, NY (hereafter FDRL).

15. Ibid.

16. "Problem of Japanese-American Relations," April 5, 1934, PSF: Japan, Box 42, FDRL.

17. "Memorandum of Conversation Between Secretary Hull and the Japanese Ambassador, Mr. Hirosi Saito," May 16, 1934, PSF: Japan, Box 42, FDRL.

18. "Memorandum of Conversation between Secretary Hull and the Japanese Ambassador, Mr. Hirosi Saito," May 19, 1934, PSF: Japan, Box 42, FDRL.

19. *FRUS* 1935, vol. 3, 831.

20. Joseph Grew to Cordell Hull, "Urge Toward Expansion in Japan," February 6, 1935, and Cordell Hull to Franklin D. Roosevelt, March 13, 1935, PSF: Japan, Box 42, FDRL.

21. Ibid.

22. Ibid.

23. William Phillips, *Ventures in Diplomacy* (Boston: Beacon Press, 1952), 168.

24. Nixon, *Franklin D. Roosevelt and Foreign Affairs*, 2: 437–38.

25. Nixon, *Franklin D. Roosevelt and Foreign Affairs*, 3: 12–14.

26. Rosenman, *Public Papers and Addresses of Franklin D. Roosevelt*, 4: 442–43.

27. Franklin D. Roosevelt to Jesse Straus, February 13, 1936, PSF: Diplomatic, Box 42, FDRL.

28. Douglas Little, *Malevolent Neutrality: The United States, Great Britain, and the Origins of the Spanish Civil War* (Ithaca, NY: Cornell University Press, 1985), 69–70, 11. Alexander Kerensky had led the government in Russia between the fall of the czar and the Bolsheviks' coming to power.

29. Bullitt and Bowers quoted in Little, *Malevolent Neutrality*, 201, 195; Phillips Diary, August 1935, William Phillips Papers, Houghton Library, Harvard University, Cambridge, MA (hereafter WPP).

30. Phillips Diary, August 4, 1936, WPP.

31.   *FRUS* 1937, vol. 1, 346–47, 352–53; Moffat Diary, September 10, 1937, Jay Pierrepont Moffat Papers, Houghton Library, Harvard University, Cambridge, MA (hereafter JPMP).

Chapter 3

1.   Bernard Baruch, "Neutrality," *Current History*, June 1936, 44.
2.   *FRUS* 1933, vol. 2, 328–30.
3.   State Department, February 16, 1937, "Memorandum for the Honorable Norman H. Davis: A Contribution to a Peace Settlement," Box 24, Norman H. Davis Papers, Library of Congress, Washington, DC.
4.   Ibid.
5.   Ibid.
6.   Franklin D. Roosevelt to William Phillips, May 13, 1937, WPP.
7.   Sumner Welles, "Trade Recovery Through Reciprocal Trade Agreements," October 16, 1936, Sumner Welles Papers (hereafter SWP), Box 194, FDRL.
8.   Sumner Welles, "Present Aspects of World Peace," July 7, 1937, SWP, Box 194, FDRL.
9.   Sumner Welles, "Our Foreign Policy and Peace," October 19, 1936, SWP, Box 194, FDRL.
10.   Ibid.
11.   Welles, "Present Aspects of World Peace," July 7, 1937, SWP, Box 194, FDRL.
12.   Ibid.
13.   Ibid.
14.   *FRUS* 1937, vol. 1, 655–70.
15.   Sumner Welles, *The Time for Decision* (New York: Harper & Brothers, 1944), 50, 65.
16.   *FRUS* 1938, vol. 1, 115–20.
17.   Ibid., 147–48.
18.   Beatrice B. Berle and Travis Beal Jacobs, eds., *Navigating the Rapids 1918–1971, From the Papers of Adolf A. Berle* (New York: Harcourt Brace Jovanovich, 1973), 184–85.
19.   Donald B. Schewe, ed., *Franklin D. Roosevelt and Foreign Affairs, January 1937–August 1939*, vol. 7 (New York: Garland Press, 1979), doc. 1309.
20.   Moffat Diary, September 30, 1938, JPMP; Sumner Welles, "The European Crisis," October 3, 1938, SWP, Box 194, FDRL.
21.   Quoted in John Morton Blum, *From the Morganthau Diaries: Years of Crisis, 1928–1938* (Boston: Houghton Mifflin, 1959), 524.
22.   Schewe, *Franklin D. Roosevelt and Foreign Affairs*, vol. 16, doc. 2011.
23.   Dallek, *Franklin D. Roosevelt and American Foreign Policy*, 147.
24.   *Time*, October 18, 1937, 18.
25.   Schewe, *Franklin D. Roosevelt and Foreign Affairs*, vol. 7, doc. 524.

26. Ibid.
27. Ibid.
28. Ibid.
29. Ibid.
30. Ibid., vol. 7, doc. 530.
31. Henry L. Stimson to Franklin D. Roosevelt, November 15, 1937, President's Personal File (hereafter PPF), Box 20, FDRL.
32. Franklin D. Roosevelt to Cordell Hull, November 22, 1937; Franklin D. Roosevelt to Henry L. Stimson, November 24, 1937, PPF, Box 20, FDRL.
33. Franklin D. Roosevelt to Cordell Hull, December 13, 1937, PSF, Box 42, FDRL.
34. Schewe, *Franklin D. Roosevelt and Foreign Affairs*, vol. 7, doc. 686.
35. Ibid., vol. 12, doc. 1403a.
36. Ibid.
37. Ibid.
38. McJimsey, *Documentary History of the Franklin D. Roosevelt Presidency*, vol. 7, doc. 107.
39. Ibid.
40. Schewe, *Franklin D. Roosevelt and Foreign Affairs*, vol. 8, doc. 792.
41. Ibid.
42. Ibid., vol. 13, doc. 1503.
43. Ibid.
44. Ibid., vol. 16, doc. 1925.

Chapter 4

1. *FRUS* 1940, vol. 2, 691–98.
2. Rosenman, *Public Papers and Addresses of Franklin D. Roosevelt*, 9: 259–64.
3. Ibid., 391–407.
4. "Japan: Imitation of Naziism?" *Time*, July 22, 1940.
5. *FRUS* 1940, vol. 4, 586.
6. Rosenman, *Public Papers and Addresses of Franklin D. Roosevelt*, 9: 517.
7. Ibid., 604–8.
8. McJimsey, *Documentary History of the Franklin D. Roosevelt Presidency*, vol. 2, doc. 10.
9. Ibid.
10. Ibid.
11. Ibid.
12. Ibid., doc. 11.
13. Ibid.
14. U.S. Senate, *Congressional Record* 87, pt. 1, 1109.
15. Ibid., pt. 2, 1281–82.
16. Ibid., pt. 1, 1097–98.
17. Hadley Cantril, ed., *Public Opinion, 1935–1946* (Princeton, NJ: Princeton

University Press, 1951), 410; PSF: Public Opinion, Box 157, FDRL.

18. Henry L. Stimson, Stimson Diary (microfilm edition), April 25, 1941, Sterling Library, Yale University, New Haven, CT (hereafter HLSD).

19. Henry L. Stimson and McGeorge Bundy, *On Active Service in Peace and War* (New York: Harper & Brothers, 1947), 370.

20. Rosenman, *Public Papers and Addresses of Franklin D. Roosevelt*, 10: 181–94.

21. Ibid.

22. Quoted in Reynolds, *From Munich to Pearl Harbor*, 135.

23. Rosenman, *Public Papers and Addresses of Franklin D. Roosevelt*, 10: 314–18.

24. Ibid., 384–92.

25. Ibid.

26. Stimson Diary, October 2, 1940, HLSD.

27. Joseph Grew to Franklin D. Roosevelt, December 14, 1940, PSF: CF Box 9, FDRL.

28. Franklin D. Roosevelt to Joseph Grew, January 21, 1941, PSF: CF Box 9, FDRL.

29. See Waldo Heinrichs, "FDR and the Entry Into World War II," *Prologue*, Fall 1994, 119–29.

30. Rosenman, *Public Papers and Addresses of Franklin D. Roosevelt*, 10: 277–83.

31. *FRUS: Japan, 1931–41*, vol. 2, 546–79.

32. Memorandum of Conference Between Secretary Hull and Secretary Stimson, October 6, 1941, and Stimson Diary, October 16 and 28, 1941, HLSD.

33. Stimson Diary, November 25, 1941, HLSD.

34. Stimson Diary, December 7, 1941, HLSD.

35. Rosenman, *Public Papers and Addresses of Franklin D. Roosevelt*, 10: 514–15.

Conclusion

1. Henry Luce, "The American Century," in William Appleman Williams et al., eds., *America in Vietnam: A Documentary History* (Garden City, NY: Doubleday, 1985), 22–27.

2. Studs Terkel, *"The Good War": An Oral History of World War II* (New York: Pantheon, 1984); Tom Brokaw, *The Greatest Generation* (New York: Random House, 1998).

BIBLIOGRAPHY

Primary Sources

Archives

Davis, Norman H. Papers. Library of Congress, Washington, DC.

Hughes, Charles Evans. Papers. Library of Congress, Washington, DC.

Hull, Cordell. Papers (microfilm edition). Library of Congress, Washington, DC.

Long, Breckinridge. Papers. Library of Congress, Washington, DC.

Moffat, Jay Pierrepont. Papers. Houghton Library. Harvard University, Cambridge, MA.

Phillips, William. Papers. Houghton Library. Harvard University, Cambridge, MA.

Roosevelt, Franklin D. Papers. Franklin D. Roosevelt Presidential Library, Hyde Park, NY.

Stimson, Henry L. Diary (microfilm edition). Sterling Library, Yale University, New Haven, CT.

Stimson, Henry L. Papers. Yale University, New Haven, CT.

U.S. Department of State. Record Group 59: General Records of the Department of State. National Archives, College Park, MD.

Welles, Sumner. Papers. Franklin D. Roosevelt Presidential Library, Hyde Park, NY.

Published Documents

Baruch, Bernard. "Neutrality." *Current History*, June 1936, 44.

Berle, Beatrice B., and Travis Beal Jacobs, eds. *Navigating the Rapids 1918–1971, From the Papers of Adolf A. Berle.* New York: Harcourt Brace Jovanovich, 1973.

Blum, John Morton, ed. *From the Morganthau Diaries: Years of Crisis, 1928–1938*. Boston: Houghton Mifflin, 1959.

Cantril, Hadley, ed. *Public Opinion, 1935–1946*. Princeton, NJ: Princeton University Press, 1951.

Complete Presidential Press Conferences of Franklin D. Roosevelt, 1933–1945. 25 vols. New York: Da Capo Press, 1972.

McJimsey, George, ed. *Documentary History of the Franklin D. Roosevelt Presidency*. 10 vols. Bethesda, MD: University Publications of America, 2001.

Nixon, Edgar B., ed. *Franklin D. Roosevelt and Foreign Affairs*. 3 vols. Cambridge: Belknap Press of Harvard University Press, 1969.

Roosevelt, Elliot, ed. *F.D.R.: His Personal Letters, 1928–1945*. 2 vols. New York: Duell, Sloan and Pearce, 1950.

Rosenman, Samuel I., ed. *The Public Papers and Addresses of Franklin D. Roosevelt*. 13 vols. New York: Random House, 1938–50.

Schewe, Donald B., ed. *Franklin D. Roosevelt and Foreign Affairs, January 1937–August 1939*. 11 vols. New York: Garland Press, 1979.

Stimson, Henry L. "The United States and the Other American Republics," February 6, 1931. Washington, DC: Government Printing Office, 1931.

U.S. Department of State. *Foreign Relations of the United States*. Washington, DC: Government Printing Office, 1931–41.

U.S. Department of State. *Memorandum on the Monroe Doctrine Prepared by J. Rueben Clark, Undersecretary of State, 17 December 1928*. Washington, DC: Government Printing Office, 1930.

U.S. Senate. *Congressional Record*. Vol. 87.

Autobiographies and Memoirs

Hughes, Charles Evans. *Our Relations to the Nations of the Western Hemisphere*. Princeton, NJ: Princeton University Press, 1928.

Hull, Cordell. *The Memoirs of Cordell Hull*. 2 vols. New York: Macmillan, 1948.

Phillips, William. *Ventures in Diplomacy*. Boston: Beacon Press, 1952.

Stimson, Henry L., and McGeorge Bundy. *On Active Service in Peace and War*. New York: Harper & Brothers, 1947.

Welles, Sumner. *The Time for Decision*. New York: Harper & Brothers, 1944.

———. *Seven Decisions That Shaped History*. New York: Harper & Brothers, 1950.

Newspapers and Periodicals

Current History
New Republic
New York Times
Time

Secondary Sources

Barnhart, Michael A. *Japan Prepares for Total War: The Search for Economic Security, 1919–1941.* Ithaca: Cornell University Press, 1987.

———. "The Origins of World War II in Asia and the Pacific: Synthesis Impossible?" *Diplomatic History* 20 (Spring 1996): 241–60.

Bennett, Edward M. *Franklin D. Roosevelt and the Search for Security: American-Soviet Relations, 1933–1939.* Wilmington, DE: Scholarly Resources, 1985.

———. *Franklin D. Roosevelt and the Search for Victory: American-Soviet Relations, 1939–1945.* Wilmington, DE: Scholarly Resources, 1990.

Bolt, Ernest C., Jr. "Isolation, Expansion, and Peace: American Foreign Policy Between the Wars." In Gerald K. Haines and Samuel Walker, eds. *American Foreign Relations: A Historiographical Review.* Westport, CT: Greenwood Press, 1981.

Borg, Dorothy. "Notes on Roosevelt's Quarantine Speech." *Political Science Quarterly* 72 (September 1957): 405–33.

Boyce, Robert, and Joseph A. Maiolo, eds. *The Origins of World War Two: The Debate Continues.* Houndmills, Basingstoke: Palgrave Macmillan, 2003.

Brokaw, Tom. *The Greatest Generation.* New York: Random House, 1998.

Burns, James MacGregor. *Roosevelt: The Lion and the Fox.* New York: Harcourt, Brace, and World, 1956.

Clifford, J. Garry. "Both Ends of the Telescope: New Perspectives on FDR and American Entry Into World War II," *Diplomatic History* 13 (Spring 1989): 213–30.

Cole, Wayne S. *America First: The Battle Against Intervention, 1940–1941.* Madison: University of Wisconsin Press, 1953.

———. "American Entry Into World War II: A Historiographical Appraisal," *Mississippi Valley Historical Review* 43 (March 1957): 595–617.

———. *Roosevelt and the Isolationists, 1932–1945.* Lincoln: University of Nebraska Press, 1983.

Dallek, Robert. *Franklin D. Roosevelt and American Foreign Policy, 1932–1945.* New York: Oxford University Press, 1979.

Divine, Robert. *The Illusion of Neutrality: Franklin D. Roosevelt and the Struggle Over the Arms Embargo.* Chicago: University of Chicago Press, 1962.

———. *The Reluctant Belligerent: American Entry Into World War II.* 2nd ed. New York: Wiley, 1972.

———. *Roosevelt and World War II.* Baltimore: Johns Hopkins University Press, 1969.

Doenecke, Justus D. "Beyond Polemics: An Historiographical Re-Appraisal of American Entry Into World War II," *History Teacher* 12 (February 1979): 217–51.

————. *Storm on the Horizon: The Challenge to American Intervention, 1939–1941*. Lanham, MD: Rowman and Littlefield, 2000.

————. "U.S. Policy and the European War, 1939–1941," *Diplomatic History* 19 (Fall 1995): 664–98.

————, and John E. Wiltz. *From Isolation to War, 1931–1941*. 3rd ed. Wheeling, IL: Harlan Davidson, 2003.

————, and Mark A. Stoler, *Debating Franklin D. Roosevelt's Foreign Policies, 1933–1945*. Lanham, MD: Rowman and Littlefield, 2005.

Engelbrecht, Helmuth Carol, and Frank Cleary Hanighen. *Merchants of Death: A Study of the International Armament Industry*. New York: Dodd, Mead & Company, 1934.

Farnham, Barbara Rearden. *Roosevelt and the Munich Crisis: A Study of Political Decision-Making*. Princeton, NJ: Princeton University Press, 1997.

Fousek, John. *To Lead the Free World: American Nationalism and the Cultural Roots of the Cold War*. Chapel Hill: University of North Carolina Press, 2000.

Gardner, Lloyd. *Economic Aspects of New Deal Diplomacy*. Boston: Beacon Press, 1971.

————. *Spheres of Influence: The Partition of Europe From Munich to Yalta*. Chicago: Ivan R. Dee, 1993.

Haines, Gerald K. "Roads to War: United States Foreign Policy, 1931–1941." In Gerald K. Haines and Samuel Walker, eds. *American Foreign Relations: A Historiographical Review*. Westport, CT: Greenwood Press, 1981.

Hamby, Alonzo. *For the Survival of Democracy: Franklin Roosevelt and the World Crisis of the 1930s*. New York: Free Press, 2004.

Harris, Brice, Jr. *The United States and the Italo-Ethiopian Crisis*. Stanford, CA: Stanford University Press, 1964.

Hearden, Patrick J. *Roosevelt Confronts Hitler: America's Entry Into World War II*. DeKalb: Northern Illinois University Press, 1987.

Heinrichs, Waldo. "FDR and the Entry Into World War II." *Prologue*, Fall 1994, 119–29.

————. *Threshold of War: Franklin D. Roosevelt and American Entry Into World War II*. New York: Oxford University Press, 1988.

Hogan, Michael. *A Cross of Iron: Harry S. Truman and the Origins of the National Security State, 1945–1954*. Cambridge: Cambridge University Press, 1998.

Iriye, Akira. *The Origins of the Second World War in Asia and the Pacific*. New York: Longman, 1987.

Jablon, Howard. *Crossroad of Decision: The State Department and Foreign Policy, 1933–1937*. Lexington: University of Kentucky Press, 1983.

Kennedy, David M. *Freedom From Fear: The American People in Depression and War, 1929–1945*. New York: Oxford University Press, 1999.

Kimball, Warren. *Forged in War: Roosevelt, Churchill, and the Second World War.* New York: William Morrow, 1997.

————. *The Juggler: Franklin Roosevelt as Wartime Statesman.* Princeton, NJ: Princeton University Press, 1991.

————. *The Most Unsordid Act: Lend-Lease, 1939–1941.* Baltimore, MD: Johns Hopkins University Press, 1969.

Langer, William L., and S. Everett Gleason. *The Challenge to Isolation: The World Crisis of 1937–1940 and American Foreign Policy.* 2 vols. New York: Harper & Row, 1952.

————. *The Undeclared War, 1940–1941.* New York: Harper & Row, 1953.

Leffler, Melvyn. *A Preponderance of Power: National Security, the Truman Administration, and the Cold War.* Stanford, CA: Stanford University Press, 1992.

Leuchtenburg, William E. *Franklin D. Roosevelt and the New Deal, 1932–1940.* New York: Harper & Row, 1963.

Little, Douglas. *Malevolent Neutrality: The United States, Great Britain, and the Origins of the Spanish Civil War.* Ithaca, NY: Cornell University Press, 1985.

Luce, Henry. "The American Century." In William Appleman Williams, et al., eds. *America in Vietnam: A Documentary History.* Garden City, NY: Doubleday, 1985.

MacDonald, C. A. *The United States, Britain and Appeasement, 1936–1939.* New York: St. Martin's Press, 1981.

Maney, Patrick J. *The Roosevelt Presence: A Biography of Franklin Delano Roosevelt.* New York: Twayne, 1992.

Morison, Etling E. *Turmoil and Tradition: A Study of the Life and Times of Henry L. Stimson.* Boston: Houghton Mifflin, 1960.

Nobutaka Ike, ed. and trans. *Japan's Decision for War.* Stanford, CA: Stanford University Press, 1967.

Offner, Arnold. *American Appeasement: United States Foreign Policy and Germany, 1933–1938.* New York: W. W. Norton, 1969.

————. *Origins of the Second World War: American Foreign Policy and World Politics, 1917–1941.* New York: Praeger Publishers, 1975.

Pusey, Merlo J. *Charles Evans Hughes.* New York: Macmillan, 1951.

Reynolds, David. *The Creation of the Anglo-American Alliance, 1937–1941: A Study in Competitive Cooperation.* Chapel Hill: University of North Carolina Press, 1982.

————. *From Munich to Pearl Harbor: Roosevelt's America and the Origins of the Second World War.* Chicago: Ivan R. Dee, 2001.

Rock, William R. *Chamberlain and Roosevelt: British Foreign Policy and the United States, 1937–1940.* Columbus: Ohio State University Press, 1988.

Russett, Bruce. *No Clear and Present Danger: A Skeptical View of the U.S. Entry Into World War II.* New York: Harper & Row, 1972.

Schmitz, David F. *Henry L. Stimson: The First Wise Man*. Wilmington, DE: Scholarly Resources, 2001.

———. *The United States and Fascist Italy, 1922–1940*. Chapel Hill: University of North Carolina Press, 1988.

Seldes, George. *Iron, Blood and Profits: An Exposure of the World-Wide Munitions Racket*. New York: Harper & Brothers, 1934.

Small, Melvin. *Was War Necessary? National Security and U.S. Entry Into War*. Beverly Hills, CA: Sage Publications, 1980.

Smith, Daniel M. *The Great Departure: The United States and World War I, 1914–1920*. New York: Wiley, 1965.

Terkel, Studs. *"The Good War": An Oral History of World War II*. New York: Pantheon, 1984.

Utley, Jonathan. *Going to War With Japan, 1937–1941*. Knoxville: University of Tennessee Press, 1985.

Williams, William A. *The Tragedy of American Diplomacy*. 2nd rev. ed. New York: Dell, 1972.

INDEX

ABOUT THE AUTHOR

DAVID F. SCHMITZ is the Robert Allen Skotheim Chair of History at Whitman College. He is the author of *The United States and Right-Wing Dictatorships, 1965–1989*; *Thank God They're on Our Side: The United States and Right-Wing Dictatorships, 1921–1965*; *Henry L. Stimson: The First Wise Man*; *The United States and Fascist Italy, 1922–1940*; and *The Tet Offensive: Politics, War, and Public Opinion*; and he is the editor, with Richard D. Challener, of *Appeasement in Europe: A Reassessment of U.S. Policies*; and the editor, with T. Christopher Jespersen, of *Architects of the American Century: Individuals and Institutions in Twentieth-Century U.S. Foreign Policymaking*.